A BRIEF SILENCE

A Brief Silence

A MEMOIR

SHEILA RUBY

Sheila Ruby
A Brief Silence: A Memoir

Publisher: Sheila Ruby
Text Design: Angela Jiniel LaMunyon
Cover Design: Angela Jiniel LaMunyon
Developmental Edits: Kristen Hamilton
Copy and Line Editing: Sheila Ruby

A CIP record for this book is available from the Library of Congress Cataloging-in-Publication Data

ISBN-10: 979-8-218-12553-0

In Loving Memory of:

Sarah Sodd

Debbie Gottschalk

Christena Mohr

All names in this story have been changed to protect the privacy of the individuals - with the exception of my name and my brother Damien.

CHAPTER 1

I think back to a particular day in my life, a specific time, and it amazes me how clearly I can see it all unfold. Like I wasn't experiencing it, but witnessing it from outside my body, looking down.

It was a typical June day.

I was a full-time college student just a few weeks into the summer semester. For about a year, I had been out of the military and taking classes at a nearby community college.

Before I even got out of bed, the sun was already shining through the windows and lighting up the house. I didn't have classes that day, which was good because I woke up feeling emotional and drained.

As soon as I woke up, I had memories come back all at once. I woke up that morning and saw the faces of people in my mind that I wished weren't there. The smell of peaches came back to me, even though there were none actually there. As a kid, I used things like that to hold onto memories. I picked a scent, or a word, or something I had seen, and replayed it in my head for days at a time. That was my routine when I had a day or a memory that I wanted to hold onto. I was always so afraid of forgetting.

The peaches weren't especially significant, but it opened the gate, and allowed so many more memories to flood back in.

Some days, things would come back, and everything would feel real again.

Quentin had been up for a while, and came to my bedroom to snuggle in bed with me. He got up and went to the living room to play. I got up and followed him.

He looked at me, and with his sweet, nasally voice, said, "Mom, I wan op-i-meal."

I walked into the living room, and the sun was shining through the curtains and blinds on the windows. That perfect morning sun brought yellow beams of light into the house. I could see the dust particles floating in the long stretches of light. I stood for a minute, looking at the dust, and watched it float as if the light was holding it there, suspending it in nothingness.

Watching the dust floating in the air brought more memories. I spent countless hours as a kid laying on the floor of the room, watching the dust in the stretches of light.

The house I lived in at the time with my boyfriend, Joe, was older, but I loved everything about it. It was a large two-story house in town. The house had an old, worn-out look to it, but it was perfect for what we needed.

There was a covered front porch. The driveway was to the right of the house and stretched to the attached garage on the back of the house and then even further behind that. The backyard was small, with a large tree in the middle, and fenced in with a chain-link fence. Next to the driveway was a six-foot privacy fence the neighbors put up that marked the end of our property.

The living room was outside my bedroom, across the hallway on the first floor. A doorway behind that room opened up to what was likely intended to be a dining room. Cole and Quentin took it over and used it as a second living room and a playroom.

I had a million thoughts running through my head that morning and I couldn't get rid of them.

Get it together, Sheila. Quit thinking about all of this stuff.

After Quentin finished eating the oatmeal I made for him for breakfast, he got up from the table and went off to play. I cleared up his breakfast and headed to the living room.

I got some toys out for Quentin and put on his favorite t.v. show. Once he was playing, I walked into the next room and went straight to my desk against the wall, knowing what I was looking for. I bent over and tucked my messy, curly hair behind my ears. I opened the larger bottom drawer and retrieved a binder hidden underneath piles of paperwork and old documents.

I looked at the binder for a moment as I sat in silence.

You should probably just put this back and find something else to do.

Then, I focused on the face of the girl on the front of the binder, behind the plastic covering.

I only looked at this binder every so often, and every time I looked at that face in the picture on the front, my heart would get heavy inside my chest. As I looked at it then, it got harder for me to breathe. I always felt like that binder held secrets inside I was not supposed to know, and certainly not supposed to acknowledge.

Looking into the big, dark-blue eyes of the little girl staring straight back at me, I remembered what pain was in there, pain no one would ever know. I looked into her eyes intensely and tried my hardest to remember that day, what I was like then, and what I was thinking at that moment.

I found nothing, though.

The girl I am looking at is smiling, and she looks happy, but I don't understand how that can be.

I was only five years old in that picture. In the photo, I had a beautiful, light church dress on and my curls were tamer than normal. I still remembered the day before the photo was taken. Still, I tried to remember that specific day, but there was nothing there. *Why did you let yourself forget so much?*

The large, soft curls framed my face. My hair did not quite come to my chin, and the style perfectly fit my face. I had pen marks scribbled deep across the face in the picture, but not enough to distort it. I pulled the picture out of the front cover of the binder and ran my fingers along the deep grooves of the pen marks.

Scars I created myself.

The day I did that, I was around seven years old. I got so angry that I started destroying photos in my Life Book. This picture was the first one that I had ruined. Every time I looked at that picture, a sickening feeling welled up inside me. The mere thought of it was enough to evoke a wave of painful memories. I had to look at this picture most of my life and remember what I went through that year. I don't know how I survived it.

With my eyes closed, I covered the face in the photo with my hand and tried to imagine the face of the little girl I had almost forgotten. I could feel the tears running down my cheeks as memories flooded back into my mind, back into my soul. I pushed them out for so long, but that day they came back, and that day I let them.

I opened the binder and read the first page.

"My Life
By: Sheila Marie King".

I couldn't recognize the handwriting on the page as I read the words. I had looked at that page hundreds of times just to look at my real name. Even then, it was strange to think that I am not that person anymore.

Sheila King died so many years ago. I felt like she had never existed in the first place for much of my life. Almost like the life I had before was made up in my head. This was the only proof I had that any of it was real.

I flipped through the first couple of pages. I skimmed through things I had added to the binder myself as I got older: likes and dislikes from my school years, letters, and notes I had saved even into my adulthood.

My social worker would add to my Life Book when I was younger. She added lists and questionnaires of my favorite things to do and my favorite memories from each family I lived with. I hated that I even had to have these. *I should've had a normal family; I deserved a normal life.*

As I got older, I would add to my Life Book on my own every year. I planned it intentionally to be something I could give to my children one day, so they never had to wonder who I was. I always wanted my kids to know where they came from, maybe because I never knew that for myself growing up.

Turning more pages, I finally stopped when I got to a photo of me when I was six or seven years old. I was with a social worker also named Sheila, whom I met at the Children's Services Bureau. There was a picture right below that one with me sitting on my birth father's lap on a couch in a place I didn't recognize.

I always assumed the photo was taken in the gas station I lived in with my birth parents, but I didn't know for sure. I looked older than I remembered being when living with him. In that photo I was wearing a 101 Dalmatian outfit. The shirt was red with puppies and matching Dalmatian spotted pants. In the photo, my attention was on something else. I was looking at something other than the photographer. That was the only photo I had growing up of my biological father. I don't know how it ended up in my binder, but it was always there. *How could he have abandoned his own children?*

My heart palpitated, and I felt an all too familiar pain as I took the picture from the binder and studied the face of the man in it. I listened to the sounds of Quentin playing in the next room as I studied the picture. I took a deep breath and, without even realizing how hurt I was, let out a sob. Choking back tears, my hands trembled.

I felt like I was suffocating, but I knew that would happen. The same thing happened every time I looked at my Life Book. It was something that I had to have, because it was a part of me, and at the same time I felt like it was taking the oxygen from my lungs every time I looked at it.

I put the picture back in its place and continued looking through the pictures, turning page after page. Tears slowly rolled down my face and dripped off the bottom of my chin. I finally stopped when I got to a particular photo that brought a different kind of pain.

It was a picture taken at Cosi in Toledo when I was the same age as the picture on the binder's cover. In the photo, I am standing with a foster family and my biological brother, Damien. Spending a little more time on the face of my foster brother, my heartbeat increased. I suddenly felt sick to my stomach as I looked into his eyes. I felt all the hate and all the pain swell inside of me all over again. Tears streamed down my face as I looked at the picture. I sobbed silently so my son couldn't hear me. I put my hand over my mouth to stop myself from crying out. *Why? Why did you give this to me, God?*

Even then, it still hurt. Looking at pictures of that family made me feel like I was suffocating. I have seen the darkness of the demons' eyes and felt the fear they bring, and I know they are real. I have looked them in the eye so many times.

I stared into his eyes and felt him piercing my soul as he had done for most of my life. As I blinked, I was the little girl again, looking at him… looking into his eyes as if he was standing there in front of me.

All the anger and hurt grew inside me.

I could feel every touch all over again, every hurt. I could feel the floor beneath me and his body on top of mine, and I knew it shouldn't feel that real, but it did. Moving on from his face, I looked at myself in the photograph.

I was only five years old, and despite what he had done to me so many times, I looked so happy. That day, and all the moments leading to the photo being taken were still clear in my mind. Every time I look at it, the memories of that day come flooding back. I put the picture back in my binder and closed it. With a heavy sigh, I brushed away the tears with my fingertips.

Binder in hand, I grabbed my pack of cigarettes and lighter from the counter before heading through the kitchen to the garage. I sat on a chair and lit my cigarette, and inhaled deeply. My entire body felt a calmness come over it like everything in the world was still and silent.

Setting the binder on my lap, I opened it again, and lighter in hand, I held up a picture. Not the one from Cosi, but a picture that I knew I needed to get rid of.

I put my cigarette in my mouth, held the photo above the flame of my lighter, and watched it catch the corner of the picture. I watched the fire work its way up the picture slowly, and the faces melted away like they were nothing.

I could feel the tears hot on my face again as I took a drag from my cigarette still in my mouth and grabbed another picture. This time I felt something good, like a weight being lifted.

Again, I watched the picture melt as I held it until it burned to the corner. I dropped it and watched the rest float softly to the ground and burn to ash.

I grabbed the picture of my birth father with me on his lap, wearing my Dalmatian outfit. Without missing a beat, I took another drag from my cigarette, lit the picture on fire, and watched it burn.

I flipped to the front of the binder and slipped the school picture from the front. I looked into my eyes through the scribble marks for a moment, hoping for something to stop me. Then I looked at the scab across my chin. I went back to that day in my mind when I got hit, and I brought the picture to the flame. And with a deep breath, watched the little girl's face disappear.

I know I need to do this, but why is this so damn hard? The smell of burning paper filled the air as I smoked my cigarette, watching the pictures become ash. I threw the butt on the ground and grabbed another cigarette.

I stood up and walked to the door, and listened to Quentin. I could hear him playing, so I shut the door and lit my cigarette. Sitting back down in the center of the garage, I gazed at the small pile of ash on the floor. Relief washed over me, but a pang of regret that nestled deep in my heart quickly replaced it.

Opening my Life Book, I flipped to the back, where only a handful of pictures remained. My tears returned in full force, and I quickly shut the book. I couldn't bring myself to destroy those memories. They had become a crutch, a source of comfort during the darkest moments of my life. They reminded me of my roots and allowed me to feel my emotions, no matter how painful they might be.

Weeks prior, I started reading my Bible, searching for answers to the questions that plagued me.

Though I thought I already knew the answers, I couldn't bring myself to believe in them. Even with the knowledge of the truth, I still hated myself, and the pain persisted.

I looked down at my now faceless binder, knowing why God gave me this. Even though I don't like the answer, I know it nonetheless.

After sitting in silence for a moment, I stood up and walked back inside, through the mudroom, the kitchen, and into the room to my desk. As I tucked the binder back where it belonged, I wished that I never had to look at it again. I walked to the living room and sat on the couch, and my son crawled up next to me and put his arms around me. I held him tighter and longer than usual.

Please, God, don't let me end up like my mother. Don't let this all be for nothing. I choked back a sob as I thought about how lucky I was to have survived... how lucky I was to have made it this far.

Sitting there with my arms wrapped around my son, I thought to myself, *Why, God? Why did you give this to me?*

This time, I meant something entirely different, though.

A BRIEF SILENCE

CHAPTER 2

I stood on the sidewalk with the acrid smell of burning wood in the air surrounding me. I watched the flames in front of me dancing violently through the front windows. A thick haze of foggy smoke suspended in the air as I watched our home being engulfed in flames.

I was in disbelief, watching everything I owned burn in front of my eyes. Everything from my life was fading away, and I was helpless to do anything. There were so many people around me on the sidewalk and on the street. Most were faces I didn't recognize. I looked around at the faces, wondering how these people were here now when I had never seen most of them before. I turned and looked at Joe, standing by my side. I could see tears streaming down his face as he watched our home burn, along with our possessions and so many memories.

It didn't hurt me the way it did him.

I had already lost so much in my life. Seeing him like that was the first time I ever saw him broken. He looked lost for the first time. Joe was usually the one to guide me, but I knew that I would have to be the one to pull him through this.

My heart dropped into my stomach as I thought about my Life Book burning. It was all I had from my early childhood and was the only connection I had with much of my past. *Please, don't let everything burn.*

Two weeks earlier, I sat in my garage trying to purge it from my life. How ironic it was that I was then watching everything burn in front of me. I couldn't get rid of everything before because it held too much, some of it bad, but it still had meaning to me. After burning some photos in that book two weeks before, I realized I needed more time to get rid of everything. Maybe God was finally releasing me from everything I had held onto for so long. The things that happened in my life without ever realizing imprisoned me. I was a hostage. People said I wasn't my past, yet I could still feel the weight of my memories each day.

Earlier that night, we had driven to the next town to drop Joe's son, Cole, off at his mom's house. It was pouring down rain when we left.

Cole had turned four years old a few months before. He was a cute, chubby boy with brown curly hair and huge, dark-brown eyes. Cole stayed with us a couple of days a week, and even though I had only known him for a little over a year, he felt like a son to me. I loved him and cared for him as if he was my child. When he wasn't with us, I would miss him and couldn't wait for him to come back.

Cole and Quentin became close, and they loved being with each other. They were complete opposites, but I think that made them like each other more. Cole was quiet and introverted, but he talked like an adult, even as a toddler.

I was shocked at the clarity of his words when I met him - it was a far cry from the gibberish Quentin usually spoke. Quentin developed speech late, and even then, his speech impediment made it hard to understand him. Cole was obsessed with everything that involved trucks and farming.

Quentin was much smaller than Cole, with light blonde hair and blue eyes, and he was obsessed with outer space and spaceships.

The streets were already flooding when we left the house and started driving to Cole's mom's house. Every so often, lightning stretched across the sky in enormous flashes, like claws tearing it open. Then, quickly followed by rumbling thunder.

I could feel the earth tremble as the lightning struck across the sky again, followed by the enormous boom.

It was early in the evening, around 6:30 p.m. Still, the sky was a dark gray, making everything around us overcast, making it look much later.

It was a short drive, maybe only 25 minutes round-trip, but the rain didn't let up at all. The drive was slow and long since it was hard to see out of the windshield with the rain pounding down. After we dropped off Cole, we started our drive back home.

Once we got home and pulled into the drive, we both knew something was wrong. One of the largest limbs on the fully grown tree stretching over our backyard had cracked in half. I could see that it had landed on the power lines going into our home and ripped them out from the side of our house.

We pulled into the flooded drive, and I noticed the tree limb and the power lines strung through the water that flooded our driveway. *What the hell happened?*

I told Joe to look as he put the car in park. He leaned forward to get a better view of what I was pointing at, and as he jumped out of the car, he yelled back, "Stay here!"

I watched as he ran to the back of the house, where we usually walked inside, through the garage. In a few steps, splashing through huge puddles, he was through the back door and inside. He didn't come back out right away, so after a few minutes, I went inside since I could see smoke rolling out of the garage's back door. I knew there was a fire.

I left Quentin in the car and ran to the front door. I walked inside and called out to Joe when I entered. He yelled something back, but I could barely hear him. The living room had a light fog of smoke. *My Life Book!*

The power was out, and I could barely see, so I covered my mouth and ran to the next room. It was too dark; the smoke was thick. I was afraid of going too far and not being able to get back out. Once I got through the living room, I decided not to risk it in case the smoke got worse or the fire made to the front of the house. I turned back and hurried for the front door, retracing my steps.

I ran through the deep water on our sidewalk leading to the driveway, got in my car, and grabbed my cell phone. *If I call 9-1-1 for the fire department, they could get here soon, and then maybe they can put out the fire.* I stepped out of the car looking for Joe and saw him running across the street to his friend Brody's house. I knew something was wrong. He still had not even stopped to say anything to me. I had no idea how destructive the fire was, but I knew he would not be running across the street to his friend's house if something wasn't wrong.

"Wat happ'n?" Quentin asked in his small, raspy voice. He was still buckled in his carseat, and I could see the look of confusion on his face.

"It's okay, Quentin. There's a fire in the house, but it will be okay," I reassured him. Smoke was now creeping lightly through the open front door. The air was feeding the fire, and it was slowly growing.

I looked down at my phone and dialed 9-1-1.

"What's your emergency?"

"My house is on fire. I need the fire department here." I could hear a slight quiver in my voice as I spoke.

I looked out my car window and saw my neighbor, Mr. Collins, who used to be my principal in middle school. He was running through my front yard in the pouring rain and signaling for me to follow him. I got out of my car and grabbed Quentin out of his carseat. Holding Quentin, I ran through the flooded yard to my neighbor's house, drenching my shoes as I ran through the large puddles.

"Did you call 9-1-1 yet, Sheila?"

"Yes, they're on their way," I responded.

"Do you need to call your parents?"

"Yes, I need to tell my parents. I haven't tried to call them yet," I responded, blinking hard to push my tears back before they started overflowing.

I grabbed my phone out of my pocket and called my dad. As soon as he picked up the phone, I could feel the tears rolling down my cheeks. The situation didn't hit me until I was on the phone with my dad. My parents somehow always had that effect on me. I knew my dad would know what to do and help me through this.

"Dad, my house is on fire! The fire department is on its way, but I don't know what to do. I have Quentin with me."

"Do you want me to come get Quentin and bring him back to my house?"

"Yes, I don't want him to see this. I'm next door at Mr. Collin's house."

"I'm on my way!"

We said goodbye to each other and hung up.

I held Quentin in my arms as I heard the sirens grow louder. They were finally coming to the house after what seemed like forever. Joe ran into the neighbor's house, where I was waiting, and told me the fire trucks were there. He asked me what I did with the fire extinguisher because he couldn't find it, and I told him I didn't know where it was. I couldn't remember where I put it.

A few weeks earlier, I started gardening. I had covered all the kitchen counters in cut-down bottles and milk jugs where I had planted vegetables. Since I needed the counter space, I moved the fire extinguisher. I thought for sure I had put it under the kitchen sink, but Joe said he looked there and couldn't find it. Joe looked visibly agitated that I had moved the fire extinguisher, and I felt so stupid for doing that.

I looked out the neighbor's door as I saw the fire trucks pull up in front of our home. I walked out onto the porch, following Joe, and watched as the firefighters started piling out of the trucks.

The pitter-patter of raindrops on the roof slowed to a drizzle, and the once-gray sky lightened, revealing a faint orange glow on the horizon. It was already 8:30 p.m. by the time Joe and the firefighters stepped outside. Joe walked down the steps to show them where the fire had started. After the firefighter grabbed the handle on the garage door, he walked back to the sidewalk.

Joe was standing by the firetruck when the firefighter walked up to him.

"What happened? Did you find anything inside?"

The firefighter turned to him and shook his head.

"I can't go inside because the house is electrified," he said. "It shocked me when I touched the door handle. It would be unsafe for anyone to enter the house until Toledo Edison can come out and disconnect the power."

"I was in the house already, and it was fine. I didn't get shocked," Joe told him.

Joe's heart sank as he realized the firefighters would not enter the house. They would have to wait for Toledo Edison to arrive before they could even assess the situation. He looked up at the sky, hoping for a ray of light to pierce through the clouds, but the world remained shrouded in a dreary blanket of gray.

The firefighter looked at him with a serious face, "You are lucky it didn't electrocute you when you walked through the water with the live lines."

He instructed Joe to stay on the sidewalk where it was safe, and he told him not to come near the house again.

Within minutes, my dad pulled into the driveway of Mr. Collin's house. He hurried over to me, concern etched on his face. "Are you okay? What's happening?" he asked.

I stood frozen, my eyes darting around as the chaos outside unfolded before me. My mind raced, searching for a way to help, but I felt completely helpless. I looked at my dad, "Quentin's inside," my voice trembling as I spoke. "I don't know what to do."

My dad nodded and pushed past me into the neighbor's house. He emerged a moment later with Quentin in his arms. "I've got him," he said. "We'll keep him as long as we need to."

Quentin was still confused. "We go home?"

I could see the concern in his eyes, and I knew he wanted more than anything to be home.

Joe's dad and brother showed up a few minutes after my dad left and met us on the sidewalk across the street from our house.

Tears streamed down Joe's face as he looked at his dad. His voice filled with emotion as he said, "They are just letting it burn!"

I wanted to scream, and demand that they do something, but I knew it was useless. It was out of my hands now.

We both turned around and saw the firefighters breaking the windows. I didn't realize it until Joe said something, but they turned it into a controlled fire. They were feeding it oxygen so it could slowly burn.

After about two hours, the power company still had yet to show up. People who lived around us had come and gone. Some stayed longer than others to watch. After standing out there for over two hours, we decided there was no point in watching the fire that was still going.

Joe grabbed the American flag we had hanging on our front porch, and he stood on the sidewalk holding the only thing he had been able to save. I stood there looking at him, wishing I could take all the pain away. I knew he had lost nothing like this before.

I was tired and wanted to get some sleep. It was around 10:30 p.m. when we finally left, leaving a crowd in the street and on the sidewalk still watching. I looked back at the house one last time, knowing there was no saving it now, but praying something would give, and they could salvage some of it.

Our house was still standing, and from the outside, you could not tell a fire was burning the inside to ash. Thinking about my Life Book burning, and my early childhood memories and keepsakes inside that book burning, I suddenly realized I was free from it.

I knew then it was probably gone.

I secretly hoped it was. It had held on to me for so long, like a parasite draining me from time to time, reminding me of so much pain that I wished I didn't have. I didn't know how it was possible, but there was a side of me that felt broken knowing that my Life Book was gone. At the same time, there was a side of me that was so relieved.

We got in my car, which was now parked on the street, and drove to my parent's house to let them know our plan. I had an exam in the morning at the college, and I couldn't afford to miss it. I needed to get some sleep. We stopped at my parent's house for a minute so I could check on Quentin.

We had friends who lived down the street from our house, and they had space for us to sleep there. I told my parents I would come back and get Quentin after my test in the morning. Joe and I drove to our friend's house in silence. When we got there, we both showered since we smelled terribly of smoke. I stood in the shower feeling the hot water beating down on my skin. The water flowing over my body felt good, but I still had the smell of my burning house on my skin and in my hair. I tried to wash it away, but even after I got out of the shower, I couldn't stop smelling the burning wood. The smell of the burning house lingered on both of us.

I laid awake for some time, replaying everything in my head, wondering what I could have done differently. I eventually fell asleep.

The morning came all too soon. I woke up feeling a sense of numbness from the events of the night before, and I could still smell the acrid scent of smoke lingering on my skin and in my hair. After getting ready, I got in my car and drove two blocks down to see my house and found it in a pile on the ground, with only wood and charred pieces remaining. I couldn't even recognize anything. It was such a big house, but the pile of burned wood seemed so small now. *This can't be real. There is no way this is actually real.*

A reporter from the local news station stood on the front lawn, her camera trained on the charred remains of my home. The smell of sulfur mixed with smoke hung heavy in the air, stinging my nostrils and making my eyes water. It was early in the morning, and it surprised me to see anyone there. In the driveway sat a bulldozer that they used to knock the house down.

I got out of my car and walked over to the reporter.

"Were you living in this house?"

"Yes, I was. What happened after I left?" I asked, my voice shaking.

The news reporter told me that took Toledo Edison five hours to make it out to our home and disconnect the power. After that, all the firefighters could do was let the fire burn in a controlled fire. "They didn't want the house to collapse and possibly damage a neighboring house close to yours," she explained.

I looked at the charred pile of rubble that used to be my home. My heart felt like it was pounding out of my chest as I surveyed the scene before me. My heart in my chest felt too big, and it beat faster as everything whirled through my mind, making me feel dizzy. *Everything is gone.* I tried my hardest to keep my composure and remembered there was nothing I could do to change what happened. I blinked back tears that were forming. *Do not start crying!*

The reporter asked if I would answer a couple of questions on camera, and I agreed. The reporter and the cameraman got ready, and the reporter went right into asking questions. She wanted to know what I saw and how we thought it happened, and she asked questions about my family and who lived in the home. She asked if we were home when the fire started, and I answered all of her questions straightforwardly and tried to be calm even though I wanted nothing more than to shut down and retreat in defeat.

"How are you feeling? What are your thoughts right now?"
Emptiness.

I respond without giving a second thought, "It's just stuff. I'm lucky my family wasn't inside the house. Most of the stuff can be replaced."

She responded, "Yes, that is very true, and it sounds like you were all lucky you were not home when it started."

She thanked me, and someone else showed up just then, and let me know an insurance adjuster would get a hold of me at some point that day to talk about everything. Then, I got into my car and headed to the college. I cried the entire drive there. It was the first time I could process what had happened, and it hit me I did not have a house to go home to anymore.

I walked into my class at the college and walked up to my professor, sitting in the front of the classroom. The class had not started yet, and I wanted to talk to him to let him know what had happened. When I told him, he put his hand over his mouth in shock and said, "Oh my God! What are you even doing here?!"

"I can't afford to miss this test and have to make it up. I need to take it quickly and then get back to meet with the insurance adjusters," I told him.

I had already thought this through the day before. It was the summer semester, so the classes were eight weeks instead of sixteen weeks. We had an exam every other week, so if I didn't take this now, I would have to take it while studying for the next test. It made more sense to get it done and out of the way. With everything that had happened, the last thing I needed was to have to be worried about taking two exams at once.

I sat at my typical table and waited for class to start, and for him to hand the tests out. I felt stressed, but I tried my best to focus on the test and put everything aside until I left. It was almost impossible to push everything out of my mind. *This can't be real. My house can't really be gone.*

Once I finished, I walked to the front of the room, turned in my test, and left to face the reality of that horrible day.

Driving back to my house, I felt so lost and confused. I kept wishing that all of this was just a bad dream, but the more I sat with my thoughts, the reality of it all sunk in deeper.

Navigating the curvy, narrow roads of County Road AC, once an old horse trail, now paved but still infrequently traveled, required caution. Though it wasn't a main road, many people used it to reach the college from other towns, and younger drivers often sped through the sharp s-curves, creating dangerous blind spots. Despite the risks, I drove more quickly than usual, eager to return home and see my family.

After passing through Wauseon and onto County Road C, my phone rang. Joe informed me that the insurance adjusters wanted to meet with us, and I let him know I was on my way. When I reached the intersection of State Route 109, I turned left toward town, my music playing in the background.

As the songs played, I found myself overcome by emotion, crying uncontrollably. It was simply the weight of everything that had happened, everything I had lost. Memories, photographs, letters, poetry, my son's belongings - all of it - gone. I tried to remind myself that there were worse things to lose, but it didn't lessen the pain.

About two miles outside of town, I saw a state trooper driving towards me. I looked at my speedometer and saw that I was speeding. I let off the gas as I passed him, praying he wouldn't stop me. Sure enough, the state trooper turned around on the road behind me. He waited until he caught up to me and flipped his lights on.

I pulled over, eyes still red and watery from crying. My heart was racing, and I felt my face flush as I waited for the state trooper. I was so frustrated with myself for not paying attention to my speed.

He walked up to my car, and I rolled down the window. He asked for my license and registration. I handed him my license while I looked for my registration paper. He looked at my license and asked if the address was my current residence.

Hesitantly, I responded, "My house actually burned down last night. I had to go to school this morning. I was in a hurry to get back because the insurance adjusters are already waiting for me."

He looked at me with a skeptical look. He didn't miss a beat, and disregarded my comment about my house fire.

"Do you know how fast you were going?"

Yes.

"No," I lied. *Please do not give me a ticket right now.*

"Well… I registered you at 68 miles per hour. I have to write you a ticket. I'll be right back."

I put my head down, looking at my hands sitting in my lap, trying to hide the embarrassment on my face. He returned after a few minutes, and I held back tears as he handed me my driver's license and the ticket. He told me to slow down and drive safely. I pulled back onto the road, and the tears started flowing again. I knew Joe would be upset about the speeding ticket, especially at a time like this when we literally had nothing. We didn't have any money when the fire happened. I didn't know how I was going to explain this to him.

I got into town and drove a few blocks to where my house was… used to be. Joe was standing on the sidewalk with a couple of people. I parked my car and walked to Joe, the sound of the excavator rumbling in the background as it picked up piles of debris. I heard the pieces of my house crashing and cracking as it dumped everything into the dumpster. Nothing seemed real, and I felt like I was dreaming as everything and everyone around me moved slowly. *Why is this smell still so strong?*

Joe told me he had gotten there just in time to dig through things before the crew started pouring piles of debris into the dumpster. My heart was pounding in my chest so loudly that I could hear it, and I felt like I was burning up as I took in the sight of what remained of my house in the yard. I felt light-headed and nauseous as I tried to focus on what Joe was saying.

How could they do that before we even had a chance to go through and see if we could pull out anything from the pile of debris? Did they not know our entire lives were in that house?

Joe looked heartbroken.

"I found a pile of my stuff from the bedroom. My baby bear and my grandpa's Bible were sitting on top of the small gun case. They didn't burn. Everything else around it was ash."

I couldn't believe what he was saying. In a charred armoire, three of Joe's most meaningful things were recovered, with just some smoke damage. I was in disbelief as he walked me over to his car and showed me what he had pulled from the remains of the house.

He also found a few of my photos, and was able to save them, even though they had minor burns and soot on them. I was so thankful he went through the pile and looked for things, but also, I was a little jealous that he got to go through everything and I didn't.

After we left the house later that day, we went back to my parents' house. I sat down at the dining room table with my mom, and we started making a list of belongings and figuring out how much it would cost to replace everything we had lost.

We furnished our home with natural hardwood pieces that we had received from various family members and friends when we moved in together a year prior. I couldn't believe that we had only lived there for just over a year; it felt like we had been there much longer. I loved that house and the memories we had made in it. I felt the weight of losing it all too real.

A piece of jewelry that held significant sentimental value was a gold ring with a sapphire gem and two small diamonds on either side. It was a Christmas present from my dad when I was thirteen, and I had treasured it ever since. The fact that my dad had given it to me made it even more special.

The items that had personal meaning were the ones that devastated me the most because I knew they couldn't be replaced.

We talked with my parents later that night, and they told us we could stay in the camper they had in the driveway until we found another place. The full-size camper was spacious, with a large bedroom in the back, and bunk beds that the boys could sleep in.

We still had no money… which had nothing to do with the house fire. I was going to school full time, and only worked a couple of days a week waitressing. I had no money when the house burned down. We usually had hardly anything left after bills. I couldn't stand living that way, and I was disappointed in myself for being in a position where I was always broke, especially since I had a son I needed to take care of. My son deserved better.

After the fire, I felt even worse. I felt like I had failed as a mother, and I didn't know how I was going to get back on my feet and be able to care for my son.

I had worked so hard most of my life, and I was terrified that I was backsliding. The only thing I ever wanted was to give me and my kids the life that I always wished I had growing up.

I had already been struggling financially, and with my house burning down, I felt like I had failed completely. It felt impossible to rebuild a life after a loss like that.

A BRIEF SILENCE

CHAPTER 3

I was only three when my siblings and I were taken away from our birth parents by social services. For most of my childhood, I thought I remembered the day they took us from my mom and dad. I now know it must have been a memory from a different time in my life.

From the time I was born until I was removed, we lived in East Toledo in an abandoned, old gas station that was converted into a house. The image I had of my home was hazy, like a dream, but certain details stood out. I remembered a vast, open space, which served as our living room and dining room. The furniture was sparse, and everything seemed makeshift, as if we were camping inside an abandoned gas station.

I could almost feel the rough concrete floor beneath the thin carpet as I wandered around the room, exploring. There was only one other space I could remember - a small room that I assumed was our bedroom. I recalled snuggling up in a dingy blanket with my older sister when we laid down to go to sleep.

I sometimes had a memory that was more like a dream. It was one that was more vivid and painful. I watched as police officers dragged my dad away in handcuffs, and I remembered feeling scared and confused. Years later, I heard the heartbreaking story of why we had been taken away from our biological parents. My older sister's stepfather, my birth father, was accused of molesting her, and my parents had been under scrutiny from social services for years due to neglect and drug abuse.

As I reflected on those early memories, I couldn't help but wonder why it took so long for us to be removed from that dangerous situation. But the answers were murky, and I knew I might never fully understand what had happened.

My birth father, Victor, had never been arrested or charged for anything. When the incident got reported to social services, nothing happened, but my mom and dad were on their radar. Social services had been involved with my birth parents long before I was born because there were suspicions of abuse, neglect, and drug use.

At that time, the only proof they had that my father molested my sister, Laura, was the story of an eight-year-old girl.

My birth mother knew what Laura had told Children Services, and she stayed with my dad after that despite what she knew. I wondered most of my life why she had stayed with him. I didn't know the extent of what he did until much later in my life, but even without knowing the details, I could never fathom why she had stayed with him for so long.

There were so many damaging pieces to my life growing up, and I tried to avoid my past at all costs most of the time. I laid in bed so many countless nights as a child trying to hold on to memories, but so many had faded. As I got older, I realized if I didn't think about things for a while, eventually, I would forget. I started training myself to remember key things from my childhood, and I would play through events each night, forcing myself to think about things because I was so afraid I would forget all of my past if I didn't.

While I was still young enough to remember what my parents looked like, I would think about their faces every night, and imagine their features in order to ingrain them in my brain. I thought about memories I had, even the painful ones, and played through them night after night so I could hold on to them forever. Some memories were already lost forever before I started doing that. It wasn't surprising since I was so young that I forgot so much before leaving my parents.

I was in my thirties when one of my sisters told me that my mom had been a prostitute. My oldest sister, on my father's side, told me that my birth mom worked at truck stops as a prostitute. So many thoughts ran through my head as my sister talked to me.

How have I never pieced this together myself? Of course, it makes sense that Beverly was mixed up in that life. Was I really dumb enough to believe that she had just had so many boyfriends to have all of my siblings? I can't believe I didn't ask more questions growing up.

I don't know why I never asked my siblings how our mom met their dads. Come to think of it, I don't know how my dad met Beverly. It couldn't have been at a truck stop… I don't think. My dad wasn't a truck driver; he was a construction worker.

Oh my God, was my real dad a truck driver? Why have I never asked anyone what my birth parents did for work? I assumed Beverly didn't work at all because I knew she was living off of food stamps. At least I think she was. Who even told me about the food stamps and the welfare?

Who told me that Victor was a construction worker? I remember telling other people he was a construction worker, but was any of that even true? How did I never put it together that Beverly was a prostitute?

My sister also told me she had suspicions that my mom was grooming my other sister Laura to be a prostitute as well. I felt sick to my stomach when I heard the words. I couldn't believe what I was hearing, and my heart started tightening in my chest as I pictured my little sister as a little girl, and how trapped she must have felt living with our mother.

My older sister Laura looked so much like our mother. She always reminded me of our mom growing up. Laura had the same blonde hair, but wavy instead of curly. They both had rounder-shaped faces and similar physiques. My birth mom was about my height, a little over five feet, and heavy-set. My sister Laura was around the same height as well. She had the same blue eyes we all inherited from our birth mother's side of the family. Laura had the lightest eyes, though, not dark blue like mine. Hers were like the sky on the brightest day, light blue and piercing.

My older sisters were way more talkative than I ever was. They were talkers, and they talked a million miles a minute sometimes, and I could tell when talking to them their minds were all over the place. They moved from subject to subject and left me wondering how we even got to the conversation we were in.

When social services took us away, Laura went to live with her birth father, who lived not too far from my second foster family, the Gadjovichs.

Despite the distance, Laura often rode her bike down the street to visit me, our brother, and our other sisters. Her visits were always the highlight of my day, filled with laughter and adventure.

One summer day, while we were living with the Gadjovichs, Laura paid us a surprise visit. We spent hours playing outside together with my other sister, Jamie. As we sat on the front porch one day, Jamie and Laura sat across from me, and we talked and laughed. After we sat there for a while, Laura and Jamie decided to start helping me learn to pronounce words I struggled with.

I looked at them sitting across from me with their blonde hair and blue eyes, and Laura said to me again, "Sheila, try again, say *CAR*."

"*Cow*," I said with as much effort as I could. Both of my sisters laughed. Jamie looked at me after she stopped laughing and said, "No, Sheila. You are saying *COW*, not *CAR*! You need to do the *ar* at the end!"

I tried again, a little slower, "Caww," confident I had it that time.

My sisters threw their heads back as they laughed hysterically. After they stopped laughing long enough to talk, they had me try it again and again until I got close enough to something that sounded like *CAR*. Then, they moved on to work with me on another word.

Laura told me her story the summer before I turned thirty. I didn't realize until I talked to my other sister years later that Laura had left out so much about Beverly.

One day, I stopped by Laura's house when she moved to a place near me. I hadn't seen her in years, and I wanted to have a relationship with her. That day I was excited as I drove to her new house. I couldn't wait to see her again, and to talk to her and hear about how her life had been going. Once we got to her house, Joe had the kids stay outside and play while he made small talk with my sister's boyfriend. Laura gave me a tour of the house, and we talked as she walked me through her new home.

I loved hearing about her life, and it made my heart swell with happiness to physically see her and see that she was doing okay. We made it back to the living room and our conversation shifted to my birth dad.

Everything I had believed for most of my life was not even real. Most of what I knew about my birth family was inaccurate. I was so young when social services took me from them, and I only had two solid memories from when I lived with them. I explained what I remembered about the day they took us away to Laura, and after I had told her, she informed me I had the wrong information.

"The memory of us being taken away has always felt more like a dream, probably because it was not what happened. I am guessing someone put the idea in my head once as a kid, and I didn't know any different, so I let myself believe it," I told her.

"You were so young, Sheila. I am not surprised you don't remember that day. I can tell you why we were taken away if you want to know the truth."

"I don't want you to have to relive anything that you don't want to. I would like to know what happened, but if it is going to hurt you talking about it, then we don't have to."

"It's okay. It does hurt to talk about it, but I don't mind talking about it at all," Laura said.

What my sister told me that day was much worse than what I had ever imagined happening. I could see it in her eyes as she sat in her living room, recounting her childhood with our mother and my father. She was reliving something that happened long ago that had haunted her most of her life, a feeling I knew all too well.

There was no doubt in my mind what she remembered was how it happened. She gave specific details about what Victor made her do when no one else was home. As she told the story, I could see the pain in her eyes. In that moment, I could see that it was hard for her to comprehend what happened to her, and then, as a result, what happened to all of us. I knew she struggled with knowing if she did the right thing by telling someone what Victor was doing to her. There was overwhelming despair in my heart for this woman, who was once a child who had her childhood and innocence taken and ruined by my father.

As Laura told more of the story, she cried. Seeing her in so much pain made me cry. After she recounted the days leading up to us being removed, I put my arms around her and held her as we both cried. I wanted so badly to take it all away from her.

God, if there is any way for you to take her pain and give it to me, I will take it in a heartbeat. I promise you; I am strong enough to handle it. Don't let her feel broken anymore. It isn't fair that she had to go through this pain; she didn't deserve anything Victor did to her.

After a couple of minutes, we both regained our composure, and Laura told me she didn't hate Victor, despite everything he had done. She recounted a discussion she had with him when she found out he was out of prison a year earlier.

Laura confronted him and asked him about what he did to her. When she asked him, he denied everything, and told her he had never done anything to her. Laura told me she thought she was crazy and had made the whole thing up in her head. She was a child; how could she have even known about any of the things she told me when she was that little?

Laura explained to me that after a second call to social services about my father, that was it. They called Beverly and asked her to bring all of us kids to the Children's Services Bureau. She dressed us all up in nice clothes that day and took us there. When we all got to CSB, a social worker informed our mom about a call they received. They told her that a parent had called to report sexual abuse in the home, and she could not let her leave with any of us that day. Our mom walked out of the building, leaving us behind, and went back home to my birth father. They separated all five of us and placed us in separate homes that day.

I spent the next six years living with strangers.

The first foster home I went to was for a very brief time. I don't have any memories of living in that home, but I had a letter that my older brother hid from me in his Life Book for years that was written by a foster family on my fourth birthday.

"Dear Sheila,

We enjoyed our time with you and having you live with us for this short time. You were such a bright, happy little girl and brightened our days. You were a lot of fun to be around, and you were always smiling and laughing. We hope you find a good home and a place where you are taken care of."

The date at the top of the letter read 11-11-1992. I am not sure why I left that family, but normally a child only moves to another foster home if the family sends the child back, or if CSB has found a more long-term home for that child. Either way, I left that family on my fourth birthday. I don't think I ever had a fourth birthday celebration.

Not that I would remember anyway, but I probably spent my birthday in the car with a social worker driving to another stranger's home. I did not have early memories of my social worker, Sarah, and she may have not been assigned to my case until after I left that first family. I imagined that if she had been in charge of my case, she would have not had me move families on birthday. For so long, she was the only good thing I had in my life.

The next family I lived with was the Gadjovichs. They had lived in down-town Toledo, not very far from where I had lived with my biological parents. The houses in the area were all closely built. The Gadjovichs' two-story home had a roofed front porch.

Upon entering the house, I immediately noticed the clutter in every room. Knick-knacks and decor items adorned all the mantels and tabletops. In particular, the fireplace mantel was home to an extensive collection of Troll dolls, which I loved to play with whenever I had the chance.

Living with the Gadjovichs felt like being part of a big, loving family. They took us in because they wanted to help children, and they showed us that by giving us the love and care we had been missing. I never remember feeling mournful or missing my parents during my time there.

Donna and Jim loved me for who I was. I could be myself around them, and they made me feel safe and secure. My foster dad even gave me the nickname "motor mouth" because of how much I loved to talk. Looking back, my best memories from my foster child days were with this family, who provided us with the support and love we needed to thrive.

We woke up every day, ate breakfast, and then we were free to play until lunch time. Donna was always home with us, and I loved that she was there every day. She played with me too sometimes, and each day I fell more in love with Donna and Jim.

Every day, I had to lie down and take a nap after lunch. Donna, my foster mom, would always have me sleep in their bedroom during nap time, probably because I would goof off with my brother if I were in the room that I shared with him. She would lay me down and tuck me in, and as soon as she walked out, I would start playing and find myself in another land, being someone else. I would often have little adventures during nap time, and I would pretend the bed was a boat, or a car, or a plane.

I would daydream that I was traveling somewhere far away. I would jump and roll around on the bed having the time of my life.

One day, the remote to their t.v. in the bedroom was on the bed, and I didn't realize it. I jumped up and landed on my knees right on the remote, and the t.v. suddenly turned on with the volume on full blast. I was terrified when the noise from a show let out. My heart stopped beating for a moment. I moved as quickly as I could and turned the t.v. off before scrambling to the other end of the bed where I was supposed to be and throwing the covers over me as I heard footsteps coming closer to the door.

The bedroom door creaked as someone slowly opened the door, and I squeezed my eyes tighter together, hoping whoever it was would believe that I was sleeping. Jim, my foster dad, walked into the room, and there I was, acting like I had been sleeping the whole time.

"Were you sleeping, Sheila?"

I responded in a fake tired voice, "Yeeesss."

"Let me check your eyes for sleepies."

I looked up at him, and he inspected my eyes, and the look on his face showed he was less than impressed. He knew I was lying, but he played along. He told me I could get up from my nap. I was so happy that he wasn't mad at me for lying or turning the t.v. on accidentally.

I loved the days that Jim was home and didn't have to work. He was fun-loving and playful. He always played with me, Damien, Olivea, and Jamie. One day, Jim showed us how he could wiggle his ears, and it reminded me of Dumbo. I thought it was the funniest thing, and I would climb up next to him on the couch and beg him to wiggle his ears. He would make a goofy face and start wiggling his ears back and forth, and I would laugh hysterically. I begged him to teach me, and he finally showed me how he could wiggle his ears. Damien and I would sit together and practice wiggling our ears every day until we finally figured out how to do it.

Damien was a year older than me, and I was closer to him than any of my sisters. He was my big brother, and we were as thick as thieves growing up. Damien looked more like me than any of my other siblings, despite him having a different father. His eyes were dark blue like mine, but mine were a little bigger. We both had large defined dimples on our cheeks that everyone seemed to love, but Damien's were a little more prominent than mine were. He had the same color and texture of hair that I had. Growing up, we often had strangers ask us if we were twins. We could have passed as twins, and sometimes we lied and told people we were. Despite me annoying my brother by following him around all the time, he loved me so much and would do anything to protect me. He was everything I wasn't; brave, strong, fearless, and he did what he wanted when he wanted to do it. I didn't have the guts that he did, but I followed along with any ideas he had without hesitation.

We had been living with Donna and Jim for almost a year when the accident happened.

I remember the day clearly.

Jim was a lineman who worked on power lines and he was electrocuted while on the job. I remember Donna telling us what had happened, and I felt worry boiling up in me, not knowing what would happen to Jim. He had to be rushed to the hospital, and he was there for days. The next few days were a blur. We didn't see much of Jim, but we heard updates from Donna about his condition. When he came home from the hospital, Donna helped him to the couch, and sat him down. My siblings and I climbed up on the couch next to him.

We bombarded him with questions about what happened, and after he answered, he asked Donna to hand him some photographs. He showed us pictures someone had taken of him while he was in the hospital. Before he handed me a couple of them, he told me not to show my baby sister, Olivea. He didn't want the large wound stretching across his stomach to scare her. He handed me a couple of pictures while he showed Damien and Jamie other ones, and I turned away from him and sat on the couch. I was shocked at how bad the wound on his stomach looked. His skin was red and looked burned. I could tell by the way he acted that the injury was still very painful.

A couple of days later, Sarah, our social worker, came to pick us up. Donna and Jim explained we couldn't stay with them anymore. They didn't give us much of an explanation, but I overheard Donna saying something about Jim not being able to work and her not being able to take care of us on her own. I felt devastated - I had grown attached to Donna and Jim, and I didn't want to leave.

They kept Olivea. She was only about a year and a half old. I didn't know for sure why she stayed with them, but I had always guessed that they wanted to keep her since she was the youngest. I would find out one day why they kept Olivea but not the rest of us, but as a little girl, I never would have understood the reasons. A few years later, they adopted Olivea. I didn't see her regularly after I left their home, but one day my social worker told me she had been adopted.

For much of my childhood, I had some resentment and jealousy towards my sister because they did not keep me too. I wished they had picked me instead of her. Maybe they thought there was still a chance for her to grow up unharmed and live a normal life; perhaps it was already too late for the rest of us.

There was always this stigma around foster kids that I realized as I got older. Every year spent in foster care, the chances of being adopted lowered.

When I was in my twenties, Olivea called me one day and told me that her mom, Donna, had lung cancer. Donna and Jim had been smokers. As Olivea told me the news, I had flashbacks of living with them. I remembered how their house always smelled like cigarettes. There was always an ashtray on the coffee table in front of the couch, and Donna and Jim usually had cigarettes in their mouths. As a little girl, I didn't think much of it - lots of people smoked back then.

When Olivea had called me, she told me that Donna had already been doing chemo for a while, and she didn't know if she would be around for much longer. I felt a lump form in my throat as I thought about Donna - she had always been a tough woman, but cancer was a formidable opponent. I could hear the fear and sadness in Olivea's voice, and I knew I had to be there for her.

The next week, I went to visit Donna, and Joe went with me. He knew how important Donna and Jim were to me, and I wanted him to meet both of them. I was heartbroken when I walked inside and saw Donna in a wheelchair. She looked frail and weak- nothing like how I remembered her as a child. Being around Donna and Jim gave me a sense of nostalgia, and I was happy that even after so many years, I still looked at them and saw the first people who were like parents to me. We sat and talked with Donna, Jim, and Olivea for a while, and Donna told me how much she loved me and how much she had wished we could have all stayed with her. I told her and Jim that I had always considered them my mom and dad, even after I left their home. They were the first genuine experience I had with parents who showed unconditional love.

A few months later, she passed away. At her funeral in January 2013, Joe and I stood in the church where the funeral was being held. Olivea noticed me right away and walked up to me. We talked for a few minutes, and then Jim walked up and greeted us. I gave Jim a big hug, and I had a feeling of being home again. We stood there and talked a little longer, and we shared memories we had of Donna. Memories were flooding back as Jim told us some stories of when I still lived with them.

Jim turned to Joe and chuckled as he said, "The thing I remember the most about Sheila is how much she talked."

He laughed to himself again, and said, "One time, she asked Donna over and over if Donna was mad at her. Sheila stood at Donna's feet while she was doing dishes and said, 'Donna, are you mad?' Sheila asked her at least ten times. Donna turned to Sheila and said, 'No, but if you ask me one more time, I will be!' Sheila was always doing stuff like that!"

Jim told us I was always like that when I lived with him and Donna. I was always worried about what others thought and worried that someone was upset with me. All my life I was aware of their love for me and my brother and older sister. I know it must have been hard for them to decide to keep Olivea, but they did what was best even though, as a child, I didn't think it was.

At my niece's birthday party last year, I spotted my foster dad Jim, and we ended up talking for a while. Jim brought up the time I left his house after the accident. I had never talked to him or Donna about me leaving their home in any detail, and it surprised me that Jim brought it up. I learned over the years that when you have gone through something like what I went through, most people never talk about it. A lot goes unsaid.

Jim told me about why social services kept me and Damien together. I always thought it was so I would have someone to look out for me. Damien ended up spending years as my protector, and I assumed that was why we stayed together, but that wasn't the case.

Jim recounted conversations he had with the social workers. He told me that because Damien was a boy and had some behavioral issues, CSB didn't think he stood a chance at getting adopted without me, so they kept us together.

They probably thought at his age and being a boy, it would force him to stay in foster care until he became an adult. They must have known that if he had been on his own, it would be harder to find someone to adopt him at his age. I didn't know it as a child, but every year we became a more significant percentage of the statistic together. I thank God, though, that they kept us together.

CHAPTER 4

It was warm and sunny out the day Sarah drove me and Damien to our next foster family. That day I imagined I would end up with another family similar to the Gadjovich's. It was hard when I left Donna and Jim, and it was even harder leaving my little sister, Olivea, behind. I looked at the bright blue sky as we drove to our new home. I had a lot of hope that day, and there was even some excitement as I imagined what the house would look like and what the people were like that I would stay with. If this was anything like my last family, then I knew it was going to be a lot of fun. I tried to think of it as an adventure.

Even at four years old, I could create grand adventures in my mind, and this one was no different. I was heading off to a new place in a new land, and I was excited to see what awaited me. I was a little nervous as we pulled into the driveway of this new home, but there was a bigger part of me that was excited to create fresh memories and go on new adventures.

On that sunny afternoon, when Sarah pulled into the driveway of our new home, I was ready for this next chapter.

I didn't know what to expect, but I was hopeful and optimistic that I was going to live with a nice family. We had to make the best of the situation until we could go back home to our mom and dad.

I hoped we would go back home soon.

As we walked up the sidewalk, I noticed two stone lion heads on either side of the front steps, and I felt my skin shiver with goosebumps. The lions creeped me out a bit, but I wasn't sure why. I was holding Sarah's hand as we walked up the steps, and I scooted a little closer to her so I could feel her next to me. As we approached the front door, I felt more anxious and realized I was more scared than excited. I wanted so badly to tell Sarah to take us back and not leave us, but I knew that wasn't an option, so I tried my best to push the thoughts out of my head.

A man and woman greeted us at the door, and they told us to come inside. They didn't look thrilled when I looked at them, and they said nothing to me after they introduced themselves. They talked with Sarah for a few minutes, and then Sarah told me and Damien goodbye and gave us hugs. I wrapped my arms around Sarah's neck and held on tight. I hoped to God that she would sense that I wanted to go with her. She left though, like I knew she would, and I stood looking out the window as she pulled out of the drive.

Our new foster parents, Jody and Doug, didn't say much to us the rest of the night. They showed us around the house and had Damien and I put our stuff in a room. Neither of us had much.

Everything we brought with us fit in a trash bag.

They introduced us to two boys who lived there as well, Carter and Cain. Then everyone went on with their day. The family acted very normal, and I watched as they went through the house and did things. I felt uncomfortable though, because I wasn't sure if I should talk or find something to play with. They did not give me any invitation to talk, and I was afraid if I went and found something to do, I would get in trouble for being somewhere I was not supposed to be. Eventually, I sat down on a couch near the front door and waited quietly for someone to talk to me.

There was nothing in particular that made me feel uncomfortable the first day I stayed with the Clarks. They seemed like a normal family, but no one there seemed to give a second thought to me and my brother being there. I didn't feel like I belonged there. My eyes darted around as I looked at my surroundings. I felt out of place, and that made me feel uncomfortable.

I sat for a while, taking everything in. The living room I sat in by the front door was dimly lit despite the bright afternoon sun, and I could see a dining room table on the other side of the front door. The dining room was an extension off of the kitchen, and I could see that the kitchen was fairly large. There was a second living room connected to the first living room, but it didn't look like there was much in there. The walls in both living rooms were adorned with dark wainscoting, casting an ominous shadow across the rooms. I sat, trying to make myself small and inconspicuous as I fidgeted with my hands, waiting for someone to talk to me.

We all sat and had dinner together, and then after that, we got ready for bed. My foster mom told me they didn't have a bed for me yet, so I would sleep in the living room that night.

There was a bay window in the living room that faced the road, and there were cushions on it. I was small enough to fit in the bay window and I slept there that night. After everyone went to bed, I laid there looking out the window and counting all the stars that I could see. I didn't know what stars were at four years old, so I imagined they were something magical floating in the sky.

I couldn't fall asleep and I thought about everything that had led up to this point. I felt tears forming and pooling in my eyelids as I thought about my mom. At that moment, I wondered where she was, and I wished she was with me.

Now and then, a car would pass by, and I kept count of the cars to give my mind something to do. I started thinking about Sarah, and I wished she would come back and get me. My breathing got shallower, and I took long deep breaths as tears fell down cheeks. My breath made foggy clouds on the window, and I watched it slowly fade away until I exhaled again, and watched a new cloud form.

I wanted to leave that house so much. As I fell asleep, I thought more about my mom and my sadness turned into anger. I didn't understand why I had to live with this family.

I want to go home.

I wanted to scream at the top of my lungs until someone noticed me and did something. I wanted to scream until someone would take me back home to my mom. My eyes closed, and I felt so tired as I laid there. I was too tired to do anything but lay there until I fell asleep.

We had lived with the Clarks for a couple of weeks and things were going okay. Most of my memories of the Clarks don't involve the parents at all. It seemed like Damien and I were always at home alone with our two foster brothers.

Nothing was special about this family, and I kept thinking back to Donna and Jim. I wished Jody and Doug were like them, but they were the complete opposites. I still hoped my social worker would show up any day to get us and take us somewhere else, but she never did. I tried to get used to things and incorporate myself into this new family.

I played and ran around outside with my brothers. We climbed trees outside and played other games. The Clarks had a large country house with an enormous yard. The boys and I could always find things to do when we were outside playing.

Jody had me and Damien do chores right away. She split things between us and one of my chores was to vacuum every day. The only areas they had carpet were downstairs in the two living rooms, so it wasn't that bad having to vacuum, but it was difficult. I felt awkward using the vacuum because it was bigger than I was and I hated the noise from the vacuum. Every day, I would vacuum in the mornings after breakfast, and I would look over my shoulder every couple of minutes, certain some monster was going to come up behind me and attack. The vacuum was so loud it made it impossible to hear anything approaching me, and that made me feel anxious. Jody didn't seem to care, though, and even when I told her I was afraid to vacuum, she didn't let me stop doing that chore.

One evening, my foster mom, Jody, made us dinner, and we all sat down together in the dining room to eat. The first thing she brought to the dining room table was bowls of salad. *This looks so gross!* As Jody set the bowl down in front of me, I wrinkled my nose. I sat there and stared at the salad, but didn't take a bite. Looking at the bright purple strings of cabbage and furrowed my brow in disgust as I pushed the pieces of lettuce around with my fork. I didn't say anything, but Jody must have sensed that I was not happy with the salad.

"If you don't eat the salad first, you aren't getting the rest of your dinner."

I sat there pouting and Jody repeated herself.

"I don't like salad," I said, my voice small and quiet.

"You haven't even tried it, Sheila. I am not saying it again; you need to eat it. You can sit there all night if you want, but you aren't leaving the table until you eat it."

I still refused. Even after everyone else at the table finished their salads and moved on to the main course of the meal, I sat there with my head down, avoiding eye contact with anyone else. I wanted to cry as my stomach growled, and I realized I was getting hungrier the longer I sat there. *I'm not eating this crap!*

Jody and Doug had somewhere to be right after dinner, and they instructed Cain, my teenage foster brother, to not let me up until I finished my food. I hated that they left and put Cain in charge. He wasn't always very nice to me, and I knew since they left him in charge, I would not get out of sitting at the table.

I sat at the table alone with my head down, listening to my brother and younger foster brother playing in the living room.

I stared down at the bowl in front of me. *I am not eating this salad. I don't care if they make me sit here all night.* After a while, Cain walked into the dining room and told me to eat the food, but I sat there silently, unwilling to acknowledge him.

More time passed. Cain walked back into the dining room, and he told me to get up and follow him to the bathroom. I got up and followed him, hoping maybe I would get out of eating the food, even if that meant he would take me to the bathroom for a spanking or to yell at me. *I'm hungry, but if I get through this punishment maybe Cain will send me to bed, and I can wait until morning to eat breakfast.*

Cain walked into the bathroom, and I followed him through the door. He shut the door and sat down on the toilet lid. I stood facing him, waiting for him to do something. I could tell he was thinking, but I wasn't sure what about. Finally, he told me to pull my pants down. I wasn't sure why I needed to have my pants down for a spanking, but I figured he wanted to make sure I felt it.

I pulled down my pants and underwear and waited for him to spank me. He grabbed my arm and pulled me close to him, and then he bent me over his lap. He leaned down closer to my body, and I felt his face on my bare butt as he rubbed back and forth.

With my body hanging over his legs, I stared at the floor, trying to understand what was happening. His cheeks and lips grazed across my skin, and I wanted him to stop what he was doing. I was uncomfortable with him touching my private parts and rubbing my skin. I whimpered, "Please, stop." He didn't say a word, though. Fear prevented me from telling him to stop again or attempting to escape. He wasn't physically hurting me, so I let it happen.

A few moments passed, and Cain sat up and told me to stand up and pull up my pants. He hadn't spanked me yet, and I thought that part was coming, but it never did.

He violated me in a way I would never forget.

I was vulnerable and scared and lived in a house of people I didn't know. He opened the bathroom door and told me to go to bed.

As I laid in bed, I wondered if I did something wrong or if I would end up being in more trouble in the morning because of dinner and then what happened in the bathroom? It felt wrong, but I knew I couldn't say anything.

I wasn't sure if he had done anything wrong; I just knew that it felt wrong. Even if I wanted to tell his parents, I did not know how I could put it in words for them to understand. I laid in bed hungry and feeling sick until I fell asleep.

The following day, I woke up to the sun coming in through my windows. I watched the light and thought about what had happened the night before, still trying to process if I had done something wrong or if Cain had done something wrong. Finally, I got out of bed and walked downstairs to eat breakfast. There was an island counter in the kitchen that had tall stools along it. I climbed up on the stool and sat at the counter as I normally did, silently watching Jody in the kitchen and waiting for her to give me a bowl of cereal.

Jody walked past me to the fridge and never said a word. She reached into the refrigerator and pulled the bowl out with the salad I had not eaten the night before. She walked to the counter where I was sitting, put the plate down in front of me, and stared at me, waiting for a response.

I looked down at the salad, confused.

I was trying to understand why she would give me the salad from last night for breakfast.

Time slowed down.

The next couple of minutes felt hazy and dreamlike.

I looked back up at Jody slowly until our eyes met. She had a look in her eyes that I didn't recognize. Jody seemed annoyed but also like she felt slightly satisfied about something. She put one hand on the counter and her other hand on her hip without looking away from me. Another moment inched by, and then her eyes shifted from mine to the bowl sitting in front of me.

I knew by the way she looked at me she didn't like me. Still, with everything moving slowly and me trying to process what was going on; what Jody was saying but not actually saying, I watched Cain walk behind her. My eyes shifted from Jody to Cain as he came into my vision.

He made eye contact with me as I looked at him, and he smirked slowly, closed-mouthed. I stared at his lips as he stood there for a moment behind Jody.

The look in his eyes was almost daring me to say something. Maybe he already knew I never would, and that smile showed his contentment, knowing he got away with it. I wanted to blurt it out so badly and yell that Cain did something to me, but what did he do? He didn't hit me. He didn't hurt me.

Jody, last night, Cain took me into the bathroom after you left. He made me pull down my pants and laid me over his lap like he was going to spank me. Cain didn't spank me, though. He touched me and rubbed his face against my bottom. He made me lay over his lap while he kept touching my privates.

The words never formed on my lips though, and I knew at least in that moment it was not a good time to bring it up. I was not sure I even knew what happened; I just knew it didn't feel right. Would Jody even believe me if I told her what her son had done to me the night before? Probably not, and I was stuck in that house regardless of what I said to her, and I didn't want to be in more trouble if she thought it was my fault.

As everything still moved in slow motion, I felt something churning in my stomach.

As I slowly tilted my head down to look at the bowl in front of me, I felt something hot moving up inside of me.

Before I realized what was happening, I felt the taste of vomit in my mouth, and I opened my mouth involuntarily and puked all over the counter and into the bowl in front of me.

I could feel the stinging ache in my stomach and knew it was because I hadn't eaten anything for dinner the night before. Still, there was another pain in my gut because I was sick, knowing Cain got away with what he did to me. I knew I couldn't tell anyone what had happened. I felt tears swell in my eyes from throwing up.

I will tell someone; I just need to wait for the right time. He will not get away with this. I wish my mom was here. How could she just leave me?

I could never eat a salad in my life again without seeing the dark brown eyes piercing into me and the look on Cain's face as he walked into the kitchen. I would never look at a salad again and not think about emptying my stomach of all its contents and feeling the hot, red rush of embarrassment and shame creeping up the back of my neck and onto my face.

The feeling of sitting there and looking back up at Jody and pleading to God she would ask me if I was okay or try to comfort me, but instead seeing the sickening disgust in her eyes as she looked at me. I had felt the moisture in my eyes forming into pools on my bottom eyelid, but I knew if I cried, it would only make it worse, and I would be in more trouble.

Jody took the bowl from in front of me without a word. She cleaned up the mess I had made and got me a bowl of cereal to eat. Cain had already left the kitchen by the time she sat the bowl in front of me, and then, she too, walked out of the kitchen. I felt too sick to eat.

I don't want to be here anymore...

I walked into the Clarks' home as an adult. The air in the house was musty and stale, like it had been trapped inside for decades. The floors creaked underfoot as I led my family through the dimly lit hallway, as if I was searching for someone or something. I shivered, despite the heavy coat I wore, as a chill ran down my spine. The house was silent except for the faint sound of footsteps and whispers that echoed through the empty rooms. It didn't take long for me to realize that I was at a funeral service for Jody and Doug.

As we walked through the house, I couldn't shake the feeling that something was off. The rooms seemed to shift and change, warping my sense of direction. Every time I entered a room that I recognized, it quickly changed before my eyes and nothing was how I remembered it. The furniture was shrouded in darkness, casting long, ominous shadows on the walls.

As I walked through the home, it was almost as if the walls were weeping, the heaviness of grief permeating the atmosphere. Feeling the sorrow, like a fog settling around me, dragging me down, was overwhelming. I wondered why I was there, but decided it didn't matter. I was there, and I wanted to see if I could find a sign that what I remembered was real. It was difficult to navigate through the house because the layout would be how I remembered, and then I would turn a corner and everything would shift and move as if the layout of the home was then mirrored.

None of the rooms were in the right spot, which bothered me. I was searching for something specific, a particular room, almost as if I wanted to ensure it was there. It wasn't in the front of the house, off to the side of the kitchen where I remembered it being.

The people who wandered the halls seemed in mourning, dressed in black with downcast eyes. Their faces looked blurred, like they were only half-formed memories. They drifted, as if weighed down by the same heavy atmosphere that clung to the house.

Despite my fear, I pressed on, searching for something that I couldn't name. I wandered through the twisting halls, my heart pounding in my chest. Finally, I found the door that led to the basement. The stairs were steep and rickety, and the basement was dimly lit, the flickering light casting eerie shadows on the walls.

And there it was - the room I had been searching for. It was small and cramped, with peeling paint and a musty smell. It almost smelled of decay, but I could not tell what the smell was coming from. The room was real, and that was all that mattered. I called out to Joe, leading him into the room, away from the steps. "This is the room where Cain hurt me", I said, holding back tears. "It's real; I didn't know if it was real."

When I woke up, I started crying as I laid in my bed. The memories of the nightmare ran through my mind on replay. I had never dreamt about that place before. I didn't understand why, after almost twenty-five years, I suddenly dreamt about that house and the people I lived with.

I rolled over and put my arms around my husband, who was still asleep. As I brought my body closer to him, he woke up. I was crying and he could tell. He asked what was wrong and even then, I still couldn't tell him.

It weighed so much on me to even think about it; I could never say it. I could never tell anyone what had happened to me.

Months went by. Cain molested me so often that I couldn't keep count.

One of our favorite things to do on warm nights was sleep in tents in the backyard. The house was out in the country, and the big yard was huge and had a lot of trees and bushes. We would climb trees together all the time, and sometimes at night, our foster parents would let us sleep in tents. Damien always shared a tent with our younger foster brother, and I shared a tent with Cain.

I loved being outside at night, but eventually, camping outside got uncomfortable. Cain always wanted me in his tent, which didn't bother me because I began to like him and get along with him. Some nights when we camped outside, he would lie down next to me and put his hand on me. His hand would work his way into my pants, and he would feel around.

A big part of the molestation was the grooming that came with it. Cain watched us all the time. I didn't understand what my foster parents did so many days and nights that were so vital that they left us alone with a teenage boy so often.

After spending months with the Clarks, I got used to sexual touching and talking. It became part of my everyday routine, and it got to a point where I didn't fight him or ask him to stop. After what happened the first time he touched me, I knew there was nothing I could do, regardless of how I felt about it. As a five-year-old girl, I often thought that all kids probably did this.

One day, I went to Cain's bedroom to see what he was doing because I wanted someone to spend time with me. By this time, I liked our time together. I liked the attention. He groomed me well to believe his behavior was normal and fun. Even though it seemed strange, I assumed it was just something that everyone experienced.

I went into his room, and he was looking at magazines with naked women in them. Sitting next to him on his bedroom floor, I looked through the pictures with him. I didn't feel uncomfortable seeing the pictures. It all seemed too normal to me. I asked if he wanted me to take my clothes off, and he said yes.

As I did, I looked into his big mirror in the corner of the bedroom. I looked at myself standing there after I removed my clothes, naked. Suddenly, I felt embarrassed as I looked at myself in the mirror. I felt my body get hot and changed my mind instantly. I didn't want to be naked anymore.

I turned to him and said, "I don't want to do anything anymore."

He just responded with, "Okay."

He kept looking at his magazine unfazed, and I got dressed and sat back beside him on his bedroom floor by the window. I looked out the window at the huge front yard and the fields surrounding the house. I asked him what he was looking at in the magazines, and he told me the girl was his girlfriend, and he showed me a picture of her naked, with tan skin and bleached blonde hair.

A few days later, I was taking a shower and taking my time because the heat felt great. I looked up at the shower head while I was in the shower with the steam surrounding me. I looked up as the water showered down on my face. Then, I moved my head out of the water and opened my eyes to see a Daddy Long Leg crawling down the water as it was coming toward me.

Getting out of the shower as quickly as possible, I grabbed my towel and wrapped it around my body. I walked down the hall in my towel, still soaking wet, to find someone who could come kill the spider for me. I walked down the hall a little and got closer to the laundry room, down the hall from the bathroom. As I walked past the laundry room, the door opened, and an arm grabbed me, pulling me into the dark room.

It was Cain.

He pushed me onto the hard concrete floor. He took the towel off me, and before I could even realize what was happening or give any protest, I felt his body lay down on top of mine.

I quit breathing when I felt the pressure of his body on top of mine, and for a moment, I could only feel the beat of my heart.

Then, all at once, everything around me went still.

There was no movement or sound; for the first time in my very chaotic and noisy life, I lay there with this person on top of me, and there was a brief silence.

I heard nothing, felt nothing, saw nothing, thought nothing. Seconds went by, maybe only a couple, and then I could hear my heart pounding in my ears, louder than I had ever heard it before.

My heart started speeding up fast, and I finally realized I was afraid. His body was heavy on top of mine, pushing down. I could see the outline of his body in the darkness as I looked up at him, and I could make out the shadows on his face. I put my arms over my chest as if I was protecting myself somehow and trying to not feel so exposed, laying there naked and ashamed.

He pushed something hard against my vagina and trying to force something inside of me. I felt something wet and slimy like snot, but I didn't know what it was. I whimpered as he pushed the hard thing on my privates again. Quietly, I said, "Stop."

Hot tears slowly rolled down the side of my face out of the corners of my eyes. The tears felt cool on my hot cheeks. My entire body felt like it was on fire and burning. I felt the tears run into my ears before I turned my head to the side, my eyes fixed on the thin yellow light seeping in from the bottom crack of the door. I closed my eyes. Minutes went by, and I laid on the floor and silently waited for him to let me go.

The silence is what I remember the most.

With each passing second, the silence grew louder, suffocating me. As I laid there, I imagined myself under water, drowning, as everything was still and silent around me. I felt like the air was being sucked from my body, and my chest felt tight as I struggled to get air back into my lungs.

I still wasn't processing what was happening. I was in my head and removed myself from that room. I willed myself to go as far away as I could in my mind and blocked everything out.

This is okay. It's not that bad and eventually he has to let me go. If I just lay here for long enough, he will let me go. This probably happens to girls all the time. It isn't that bad.

I thought so hard about other things and other places that I fully removed myself from my body. I wanted it to be over, but I could go to another place where it didn't matter what was happening to my actual body. He couldn't hurt me that way.

He took something from me that day, something I would never get back. That day, I went from a child to a woman for all the wrong reasons. I was different after that moment.

That night, I replayed in my head being in the shower, getting out, walking down the hallway, the arm reaching out from the laundry room. I remembered the towel falling to the floor, the feeling of the floor underneath me, the feeling of his body, the look in his eyes as my eyes finally adjusted to the darkness.

I could see him hovering above me, the feeling of something hard pressing against me, the wet, icy feeling, the silence, the tears pooling in my eyes, and finally running down my face.

The darkness… the silence.

That was it, though. I didn't let myself think about anything else after that.

The next day, I replayed it in my head again, this time tearing each moment apart that led up to it wondering what I could have done differently. I thought about every detail down to the spider in the shower. *How stupid could I be to be afraid of a spider? Something so small scared me and caused me to get out of*

the shower. Why did I only put a towel around me before walking down the hall? Why did I walk down the hall at all? I could have gotten dressed and just taken a shower the next day.

I don't know if any of it mattered, though. If it wasn't that day, then Cain would have done it another. I thought about my birth parents and wondered where they were at that moment. I wondered if I ever crossed their minds, and I realized if I did, then somehow they would find a way to see me. They hadn't seen me since I moved in with this family.

I realized at that moment that I was alone with my brother in this. I resented Victor and Beverly even more. If it wasn't for them, I wouldn't have lived with that family. If it wasn't for their decisions, Cain would have never been able to touch me. I hated my mother the most. I couldn't imagine anything that would get in the way of me and my child. Even at five years old, I knew if I was a mother, I would have never let this happen to my child.

I tried to be around Damien as much as I could because I knew Cain couldn't do anything to me if my brother was with me. He would kill Cain before he let him lay a finger on me in his presence. The thought of telling him what had happened crossed my mind. I thought about it a lot, but I was too afraid to let the words leave my mouth. If I talked about it, it made it real. I was afraid that even if I told him, he might not believe me. Or even worse, what he would do if he believed me. Even though he was only six, he had a violent streak, and he had no issues hurting people, especially if he knew they had hurt me first.

Cain doesn't have a hold on me as much today as he did when I was younger. I learned to forgive him with time. I think part of me has healed.

After moving in with my adoptive family, I went to counseling and talked through some feelings I had. I never gave details about what I experienced as a child.

Still, I always gave very vague descriptions of what happened to me. One therapist I saw as an adult told me I had developed remarkable coping skills. I had no choice, though; my only option was to cope. I often used my mind to escape places and situations and could quickly put myself in someone else's life and pretend it was my own.

We took a family trip to Cosi a few days after Cain raped me in the laundry room. Cosi was one of the more popular places for kids in Toledo. It had so many activities related to science, engineering, and technology. After going through most of the areas, we got to a part in an open space where kids could sit at different stations.

I sat at one station and started an activity. After sitting there for a few minutes, Cain came up behind me. He leaned over my shoulder and got close enough to my ear so he could whisper something to me that only I would hear. I can't remember what he said, but I felt humiliated. It had to do with the things he would do with me when we were alone. It mortified me that he said something while we were out in public. My face got hot, and I am sure my whole body turned red. I couldn't hide anything, and I hated that.

I recently connected with one of my birth sisters, and we sat together and shared stories about some things we both had suffered through as children. She knows who I am now, and she saw that I was happy, at least on the outside, and I think that was hard for her to understand. She asked me if I had to live my life all over again, would I do it without changing anything.

My answer was, "Yes."

I would take that pain all over again if it meant it wasn't someone else's pain to have. I would take the hurt all over again because through the hurt, I found out who I really was and what I could handle.

Through it all, I was able to tap into my inner strength and find myself. I have often wondered how God could let something so bad happen to someone so innocent and young. I don't think it was to learn a lesson. Still, I think every single moment.... every single moment... shaped me and molded me. Little by little, day by day, I learned so many things throughout my life, and each thing I learned shaped me into the person who I am today. I am strong. I love people, and I love them hard because I know the feeling of not being loved, of not seeing love. Through it all, I hope it allowed me to be a better person, maybe if it just means empathizing with someone else going through similar hurts. I find joy in every day, despite everything else, and perhaps my story is to show others that there can still be joy.

There are times I wish I could not like people, but the truth is, it is not who I am. I want to understand people, and I think that comes from not being understood myself as a child. I lived with several families who did not want to get to know me and decided not to like me.

I wondered often, as a kid, if any of those foster parents sat down with my brother and me and just talked to us, would they have realized that we were in pain? I wondered if they didn't like us because they saw two damaged children with behavioral issues. No one ever asked us why we were so defiant and wanted to cause problems. If any of our foster parents had tried to know who I was, they would have realized that I was troubled, and I sought attention because there was something lacking in my life.

I lost my parents and most of my siblings and I had to continue living each day and pretend that I was okay. As an adult, I had plenty of conflicts with others, and I realized I couldn't truly hate someone because I felt that everyone had a story. Many times, once I talked through my issues with those people, it turned out they were not much different from me, and I got to see a part of them that was hurt and damaged as well. I try to believe everyone is good deep down. I know that is not always true, but a lot of times it is.

There were so many days as a teenager I let my hurt consume me. I wanted to die, so I never saw Cain's face again. So, I never had to remember the smell of the house I lived in there again. So, I didn't have him sneaking up on me at night and reminding me of everything he stole from me. He stole my innocence, childhood, wonder, and joy for so long. It took me years and years of self-talk and self-healing to move past what I had experienced and understand I could still have a life after.

Once I was thirteen, it was like I finally hit a milestone and understood the severity of what I experienced. But, I didn't know how to deal with it.

I felt like I could never let a man touch me.

I always feared that I could never be intimate with a man because Cain would come into my mind.

He often does. In some of the most intimate parts of my adulthood, he was there and still is there, lingering in my mind. Most days, I push him aside and pray he will leave me alone. I have no idea how many times I've been in the shower sobbing after being intimate with my husband because this ghost keeps entering my head. I never let anyone know.

How could I?

This is my ghost and my past. I'm sure I occupy the same space in his mind as he does in mine. I often hope that he never forgets me.

As I got older, my Life Book became more of a burden. It only carried pain and heartache, but I couldn't let it go. It was all a part of me. Whether or not I liked it, that was my life. I think back now, and some of it seems so surreal, like there is no way that could have been my life. Who lives like that? How do people go through a life like that and come out okay? The answer is simple; they don't.

I refuse to remain silent and pretend everything is alright when I'm not okay. I am grateful and fortunate to be where I am today and to be alive. Despite being happy with my life, I fear I may never fully recover. The traumas I have gone through have been so overwhelming that I feel like I may never recover.

I was a victim of so much at a young age, and as I grew up, my only goal was to remove myself so far from it, it didn't feel real anymore. I had to create a life that would hide all the trauma I experienced as a child.

I was only with that family for maybe another six months after the rape, and then I was on to the next.

I never told my foster parents what their son was doing to me for almost a year, and I never told my social worker after she came to get us to place me and my brother in a new home.

I don't know why I never said anything for sure back then. I think my biggest fear is that I would be judged, and if I told anyone anything, then Cain would turn it around and make it my fault because sometimes I let him do things to me. It makes me sick to my stomach to even think that some people go their whole lives with sexual, physical, or even mental abuse and never find an escape. My heart breaks daily for people I have never met, stories that have never been told, and people who aren't even alive yet and will endure similar things to what I went through. I knew one day I would tell someone and make sure they punished him for what he did. I just needed to wait for the right time.

Damien was with me during my stay with this family. I think he knew what was happening, and there were even situations where he had witnessed some things himself.

My brother was a year older than me. For many years, he acted as my father. He protected me and watched over me. I can only imagine what it was like for him to know someone was hurting his little sister. Maybe if he had known the truth, something different would have happened. Regardless of what he remembers, I know that place damaged him, just like it damaged me.

SHEILA RUBY

CHAPTER 5

In 2018, I went to see my grandma in the nursing home to say what I thought would be my last goodbye. She had gotten bad again, and my mom didn't have any hope she would come back this time.

My grandma had been in hospice for two days when I finally got to the nursing home to see her. Sitting in the nursing home was always challenging, and seeing my grandma like that was hard. I wanted to get her out of where she was, but I couldn't. There was nothing I could do for her.

On my way to the nursing home, I picked up my two youngest brothers from my dad's house. My mom had been at the nursing home with my grandma for the last two days and had not left. While driving from my dad's house to the nursing home, I told my two youngest brothers how they needed to behave and asked them to do their best while we visited. With them being pre-teens, I figured they wouldn't be able to sit still.

I could tell they were bothered and didn't know what to think of the situation. Jax was never one to sit still, and it was difficult to take him places because especially places that confined him to one room, but I was glad he was still making an effort to visit our grandma, anyway. John was the calm one, but I knew how much he felt. He felt things in a way that Jax didn't, and with him being the youngest, I knew he would be upset seeing our grandma the way she was.

John was my youngest brother, and he was my adoptive parents' biological son. I was sixteen when John was born. About a year before my mom was pregnant with John, she came home one day with my little brother Jax.

Jax came to us on his first birthday. His mom was a drug addict and had left Jax in the parking lot of a hotel in a car seat. He hadn't eaten in days and was severely neglected. Jax struggled with developmental delays because of the trauma he had in utero and after he was born. Even though he was older than John, he didn't understand things the way John did.

We walked through the doors of the nursing home and made our way to our grandma's room, down the echoing, dim halls together. Nursing homes have a way of seeming so dreary and morbid, like a cloud is permanently over them. The distinct smell hit us as we walked down the halls to the room where our grandma was.

The last time I talked to my mom, she told me our grandma wasn't awake, but she was still hanging on. None of us knew what to expect. But as we rounded the corner of the doorway to my grandma's room, we saw our mom and grandpa sitting facing the bed, looking at our grandma in silence. As we walked into the room, I sensed my brothers' unease. They exchanged looks that betrayed their uncertainty about how to react to the situation. My grandpa looked happy to see us. As he lifted his eyes and met mine. I could see his eyes light up a little, and I quickly looked at my mom and saw that she had been crying. My mom's face was still splotchy and red from where she had been wiping tears away. I was never good at knowing what to do in situations like this.

I sat on the bed next to my grandma and looked at her as I took her hand in mine. "Granny, it's me, Sheila. I love you! I came to visit."

She suddenly opened her eyes with her oxygen mask snug around her mouth and smiled. "Oh, hi!"

I asked her how she was and told her again I loved her, and it surprised me when she breathed in deeply with her eyes closed and said, "I love you too," in a loud, forced voice. Her voice was muffled because she had the oxygen mask on. My mom knew just as well as me that she was on a high from oxygen deprivation to her brain. She wasn't in her right mind and might not have even known I was there.

Later, the nurse who came in said that many of her responses were from memory. "She hears something, and her brain knows she usually responds with this response, so that is what comes out."

My grandma would smile a lot as she laid in bed with her eyes closed. Every now and then, she would suddenly laugh. It was most likely from the combination of the painkillers they had her on to keep her comfortable until she passed and the low oxygen levels in her brain. My mom and I stayed there late into the night. My other brother Michael took John and Jax to our dad's house after a few hours, but I stayed longer.

Suddenly, she woke up and opened her eyes. She looked up and started saying, "Babcia, Babcia!" She was seeing her grandma.

My great-great grandma was from Poland, and when my grandma was growing up; her grandma did not know much English, so she mostly spoke Polish. My grandma, Rose, always talked about her and told me stories about when she would spend time with her babcia.

I looked at my mom, and she looked back and gave a heart-broken expression and said, "That is so sweet." She pouted out her bottom lip, trying to hold back tears. It was hard to see my mom in those moments.

I stayed with my mom longer as she debated back and forth if she should leave. I had offered to stay and take the day off of work, but after a while, my mom insisted I leave, and she would go home soon after me.

The next day after work, I went to my grandparents' house while my grandpa was at the nursing home. He had asked me a few weeks earlier if I would go through the pictures in their large wooden chest at the end of the bed in their bedroom and put a slide show together for her funeral service. I had been putting it off, but I needed to go.

It was later in the evening, and I went to their house and took Quentin with me. As I started going through the chest of pictures and I was taken aback by how many photos she had that I had never seen before. I learned so much about my grandparents as I went through the chest and read documents, certificates, and looked through countless photographs. My heart sank as I looked through the pictures, regretting that I never attempted to comprehend Rose and really get to know her. I spent so much time with my grandparents as a kid and we talked non-stop about our lives, but there was still so much I didn't know. I couldn't believe that I had never talked to my grandma about when she was a young adult.

Something she always said to me kept coming to mind. She always told me growing up that I could never sit still and she would say, "Sheila, you have pepper in your dupa!" I always laughed when she said that to me. I had never heard anyone say that, and she said it was a Polish thing. I would drive her crazy, running around and never staying still, but I knew she loved me no matter what.

It was so crazy to see her as a young woman. She didn't look the same at all, but she had the same face. Her eyes never changed, and neither did her smile. She was so beautiful and so happy. I sat there, picture by picture, document by document, went through everything.

I ended up spending a couple of hours there, and every so often, it suddenly hit me again, and I would break down. The pain would swell up in my chest until my chest couldn't hold it anymore and tears started falling from my eyes. I knew her time would come soon, but I still prayed this wasn't the end.

One picture I looked at for a long time, just taking it all in. My grandma had to only be in her early twenties. In the photograph, she reminded me a bit of Rizzo from the original *Grease* movie. Her hair was cut short and was as dark as night, and her frame was elegant and tall. She was sitting on the front porch of what must have been their house and smiling as she looked out into the front yard with two little girls playing. She had her arms folded across one another on her legs as she sat on the steps. That was the first moment in my life that I looked at my granny and saw myself. I had only ever known her as an old woman. I had never even thought that, at one point, she had been a young woman much like myself, staring out at her kids playing in the yard as I had done so many times myself.

I held that picture and looked at it and tried to imagine being there and being behind the camera. I wished I could have been there to experience the moment for myself. In that picture, I could see the joy radiating from her face, and it was obvious that she had lived an extraordinary life. I wanted so badly to turn back time and undo everything she was going through.

She was my best friend; my safe place.

I loved her so much and I didn't know how I was going to live the rest of my life without her.

After a couple of hours, I was still going through the chest. Suddenly, I heard my grandparents' Yorkies barking and I could hear their feet running down the hallway towards the kitchen as they kept barking. I heard footsteps creaking on the floor in the direction of the kitchen. Quentin was with me in the bedroom, so I knew someone else had walked in. I called out to my grandpa, so he knew where I was since he was likely who had just walked in. When I didn't get a response, I asked Quentin if he could go out and see if my grandpa was there and let him know I was in his bedroom.

Quentin walked out of the room and then walked back into the room after only a moment. "No one is here, Mom."

"Oh, okay. I thought I heard someone walking around. I will go take a look."

I thought for sure someone was there. My grandparents lived in town in a charming two-bedroom home with a distinct country flair. My grandpa, a skilled carpenter, had remodeled the house himself, creating an open and sunlit space. The decor was tastefully rustic, and I adored the layout. As a child, I would play in every room and have sleepovers with my friends.

At night, I'd often curl up on the plush couch in the main living room, reading my granny's collection of vintage mystery novels, until I dozed off. In the mornings, Damien and I would wake up to the tantalizing scent of pancakes and bacon sizzling on the countertop skillet. My granny had owned a restaurant for years, and she loved cooking. That was her love language.

I walked into the living room and looked toward the kitchen. There was no one there. The front of their home was an open layout so I could see everything from where I was standing and I knew there was no one there. *That is really weird. I know I heard someone walking around.*

My grandma passed away later that evening, after I left her house. When I found out later from my mom, I started thinking maybe it was her spirit coming back to her home one last time before she left for good, and that is why I heard footsteps. I thought maybe she even knew I was there and wanted to see me one last time. I always believed in things like that; angels, spirits, ghosts, whatever you want to call them.

I got a phone call around 10:00 p.m. that night from my mom. Her call woke me up and startled me, but when I saw it was my mom calling, I answered. Between deep breaths, she told me that my grandma had passed. Her breathing was strained and labored, and I could hear her sniffling in distress. I could tell she had been crying hard and probably had just finally calmed down enough to call me. I talked to my mom for a few minutes and stayed calm because I didn't know what to say or do.

None of what she was saying seemed like reality at all. I felt like I was in a dream, and the conversation with my mom wasn't real. The thought of my grandma being gone was so hard to accept. I thought there was a chance of her coming out of it. My grandma had been sick so many times before, and somehow she always came back. This time she didn't, though.

After hanging up with my mom, I called my brother, Michael. I knew this would affect him a lot. He was a huge kid; about six feet tall and roughly 280 pounds. He had a physique that was made for football, but his personality was gentle and kind. Michael's demeanor was always relaxed and composed. He never raised his voice and rarely showed any signs of distress. He was the first biological grandchild born from our mom and dad, and for that alone, Michael had a strong connection with our grandparents. I knew it would devastate him, and it did.

I talked to him for a few minutes, sitting in the dark on my bed, and tried to comfort him. It wasn't until after I was off the phone and laid down back in bed that I realized that, this time, it was real. My granny wouldn't get to see my kids grow up, or listen to all my new gossip, or tell me about her gossip when I would visit. I felt the hot tears roll down my cheeks onto my pillow.

I laid there squeezing my pillow, curled up on my side, and sobbed. Until that point in my life, I couldn't remember a time where I felt so broken and so much physical pain. As I laid there sobbing and gasping for air, my husband rubbed my back. He had been sleeping, but he woke up while I was talking to my mom and listening to the conversation. "I'm sorry about your granny, Sheila," he said.

"I don't want her to be gone," I said, between muffled sobs.

During her funeral service, a few days later, a woman I had known since I was a little girl stood up and wanted to share a memory of Rose, my Granny. Many people had already shared memories, but this one in particular impacted me. She said she would never forget that Rose always talked about my older brother and me. She said that our granny would beam when she would talk about her new grandchildren when they came to live with their new family.

I lost my breath and couldn't hold back the tears as the woman recounted the visits with Rose and how she always talked about her grandchildren. She loved Damien and me as if we were her flesh and blood. You would never know we weren't by talking to her. My grandma gave complete, unconditional love to us.

In my adult years, my mom always told me how proud she was of me and who I grew up to be. She always went out of her way to tell me how she thought I was strong and brave. I would have never chosen those words to describe myself, and growing up, she did not talk to me about those things. It wasn't until I was an adult and started creating a life of my own that she let me know how she felt about me.

It was ironic that she started telling me these things after I was an adult because it wasn't until after I had my son that I started to fear I was becoming like my birth mother and felt like I was taking steps backwards and going to places in my mind that would lead me to becoming my biggest fear. Growing up, she was hard on me and always expected more from me than what I was doing. I thought I was a coward most of the time, and I never thought of myself as strong, mentally or physically. I was always closer to my dad, and he was the one that typically gave me more affirmations and showed more affection. Even though he was not my biological father, he loved me as though he was.

My mom was a beautiful person, inside and out. She was very tall, taller than most women. She had gorgeous brown eyes and a brilliant smile with perfect teeth. Her skin was flawless, and she looked great naturally with no makeup on. She had short hair and wore it much as most moms did in the '90s. She went to college to be a social worker, which was her career for a long time. Being in her field of work, she knew what mentality you must have to go through what I went through and come out on top, not that I necessarily came out on top. I am not at the top now. But, then again, my story isn't over.

CHAPTER 6

In 2012, my sister, Olivea, started searching for our biological family. She knew most of our family on our birth mother's side, but neither of us knew anything about our birth father, Victor. When Olivea started her search, she had the names of our birth parents and that was the only thing she had to help her start the search.

Olivia spent hours each day searching through social media to find clues that would lead to Victor or anyone from his side of the family. The last time Olivea and I saw Victor was likely at a visitation right after we were placed into foster care. Neither of us knew for sure if he had ever showed up to visitations, and even if he had, it was not for very long. Growing up, Olivea and I had the same desire to fill in the missing pieces of our past.

Olivea was relentless in her search and one day she finally found someone that she thought could be one of our siblings. Our biological family had always been a mystery to us and Olivea used what little information she had about our birth parents to slowly put the pieces together.

I was in my first month of college, and I came home from school one day. I opened my phone to see a message from Olivea.

"I found some of our older sisters from Victor. Stephanie wants to know if she can talk to you."

My heart stopped, and I stared at the message for a few minutes before typing my reply. Until this point, I didn't even know I had other siblings from my biological father other than Olivea and Emily. I didn't know how to feel. I didn't feel emotional or even excited. It just seemed strange and surreal that I could have more siblings.

"Yes, that's fine. She can message me. Where is she? Did you find anything out about Victor?"

She shortly responded back, "Yes, he is in prison. I just talked to him on the phone."

When Olivea discovered a few siblings from our biological father's family that we were unaware of, it took days for me to process that new information. There was a part of me that was excited that Olivea found Victor and found out we had other siblings out there. It was fun to think about the possibilities and imagine what these people were like. I thought about what it would be like to meet some of my other siblings face to face, and I wondered if any of them would look like me or act like me. Another part of me was terrified about having these people enter my life when I knew nothing about them.

Until that day Olivea messaged me, I had no clue if Victor was still alive, let alone that he had any other children other than me and my two sisters. My mind was spinning over the next few days as I kept in touch with Olivea, and she slowly revealed the names of other siblings that she located. She ended up finding out that Victor had six other children besides us.

A couple of days later, Olivea sent me another message. "Victor wants to know if he can talk to you. I told him you might want to talk to him."

I didn't respond right away, but after thinking about it for a few hours, I finally messaged her back. "You can send him my number and tell him he can call sometime."

For most of my life, it felt as if he was an imaginary character only existing in my mind. It was unimaginable to me that he could be real, and I struggled to even contemplate the possibility of speaking to him, though, as a child, I often fantasized about being able to do so and that I would eventually find him. It was beyond my wildest dreams that it would happen.

Among the nine children Beverly had, I was one of the three girls who had the same father. I found that I shared many characteristics with those two sisters and I feel like I can relate to them.

My two younger sisters have many of the same qualities that I have, and I can see much of myself in them. Although, we grew up in three unique places, with three distinct lifestyles, I still felt a connection with them I never shared with most of my other siblings. Even though I was separated from Olivea when I was four-years-old, I never forgot about her. During the year that I lived with her in foster care, I made a lot of memories with her and I hung on to those as I grew up. I could go years without seeing Olivea, and when we finally re-united, it was like no time had passed at all.

I had a different connection with Emily, though. Emily did not remember me in the same sense that I remembered her. She was much younger than me, and we had only spent a year together in foster care. During that time, my bond grew intensely because I was like a mother to her. As I grew up, Emily occupied my mind much more because losing her was so traumatic for me.

After my adoption, I could still visit Olivea on special occasions, so I guess because of that, we always maintained a connection. Olivea was an unconventional soul who preferred to live a freer existence. Whenever I think of her, I'm reminded of her hippy-ish, liberated, caring and joyous personality.

When Olivea was little, she was a chunky toddler and had the longest hair that went all the way down to her butt. She had dimples that could make anyone's heart melt and the biggest, bluest eyes and freckles across her cheeks and nose. Although she was almost three years my junior, I always felt that her wisdom surpassed her age. She had a deep curiosity about who we were and where we came from, which drove her to research our family history.

I started talking to my other siblings, too. I was relieved that they were a little more normal than I expected. But, then again, what is normal?

My birth father was in prison when my sister, Olivea, found him and had already been in prison for twelve years. He was given a sentence of 22 years for drug trafficking. The cops pulled him over and found him with a trunk filled with methamphetamine, which he took across state lines out west from California to Colorado.

I fantasized about meeting Victor growing up. It was always something on my mind: meeting my biological parents. I think about it now; it was just part of the unknown. I had to know for sure why things happened the way they did. Honestly, now, I still don't know if I have all the answers.

I recently talked to my friend about my story and how I never got answers and didn't think it mattered. She said it matters, and people want to know what happened.

I would tell myself it didn't matter what happened because I was afraid of asking. The answers are out there somewhere. I just needed to have the courage to find them. There was a huge part of me that never wanted to know what happened when I lived with my birth parents and what happened to them after I was taken from them. That part of me wanted to shut everything out and pretend that none of it ever happened.

I was afraid that if I knew the truth, it would end up being something that caused me more heartache and trauma, and I felt I had already lived through enough. The only thing I ever wanted to ask my birth parents, I never had the courage to ask.

I was living with my best friend, Shelly, when my sister Olivea messaged me about finding more of our biological family. As I sat with Shelly and told her everything, my anxiety grew. I tried to process though all of my feelings as I talked to her, but I was still confused myself at how I felt about all of it. Shelly was excited for me, and she had known that finding my birth father was something I had dreamed about since I was a little girl. We both knew that there was a chance that he would not be a good person, but I couldn't take the chance of not talking to him, and then regretting it for the rest of my life.

A few days after my last conversation with Olivea, I got a phone call, and it was from a prison in Colorado.

"Do you accept this call from Victor King?"

I replied, "Yes."

My heart was pounding. I had dreamed of this day since I was a little girl. My sister had passed my phone number on to him, but honestly, I never believed he would call.

"Hi, Sheila. It's your dad. How are you?"

"Good. How are you doing? Olivea told me she talked to you."

His voice sounded normal and kind. He had a deep, raspy voice, but I liked the sound of it, almost as if it was something familiar to me I had missed hearing. He sounded exactly like I had imagined he would sound. I had a flashback to when I met Beverly and how I didn't recognize her voice, and it sounded distant and insincere to me.

"I'm doing okay… Yes, I talked to Olivea on the phone. I was so happy to hear from her… I miss you. I won't be able to talk for long, so if it hangs up, I'm sorry."

"That's okay… It is good to hear from you."

"What have you been doing?"

"I am going to school right now. I just started this month. I am still undecided about what I am going to go for."

A computerized voice came over the phone and said, "You have one minute remaining."

"The phone is going to hang up soon. I love you, and I miss you."

I didn't know what to say, so I responded, "I love you too."

"I will call again soon if that's okay. If you give Stephanie your address, I can write to you too. I love you."

"Okay, I can do that, and you can call again when you get a chance."

"Okay, well, the phone is going to cut off. I love you… I miss you."

"I love you too."

I took my phone away from my ear, looked at it, and started crying. It was so crazy to feel such a physical ache in my heart. I couldn't believe that after so long, I talked to my birth father. I actually heard his voice.

Sitting on the couch, I opened my phone, found my mom's name, and hit the dial button. She answered the phone, and after telling her what had happened, I could tell she was not happy with me. I could hear the disappointment in her voice. I was scared, confused, and unsure of what I felt inside.

She responded with an emotionless, "Okay."

"I am not sure what to think," I said.

"I am not sure what you want me to say. How did Victor get your number?"

"Olivea found him and asked if he could have it."

"Well, I think that was a mistake, but I guess, do what you want."

She was a social worker and had seen her fair share of toxic people. It's almost like she could sniff them out. She knew then that nothing good would come of this, but I didn't listen, and I didn't care. Getting hurt was worth it to me. At least I could say I tried.

After talking to my mom for a minute or two, I hung up, and I was so embarrassed and felt so stupid. My entire body felt hot with embarrassment.

I had thought it was amazing, but then my mom made me feel like it was nothing and it was pretty terrible. Her lack of support and the way she reacted to it had me so mad. I thought she, of all people, would understand. I think deep down inside; it hurt her that I would let someone who caused so much pain in my life walk right back in like it was nothing. *Why did I talk to him like nothing was wrong? Why did I say that I loved him? I don't even know him. Why are you so stupid, Sheila?*

I think about it now, and I feel like it was a slap in the face to her because she and my dad raised me, and I knew they felt my birth parents didn't deserve me, any part of me. I wish now I had listened to her. But, of course, I didn't, and I continued talking to him for years despite knowing that this man that called himself my dad didn't deserve to have a relationship with me ever.

After talking to him for a couple of months, I started to feel bad for him. Victor convinced me he never went a day without thinking about me. He told me everything I had always wanted to hear, but when I started questioning him more, I realized I would never get an actual answer from him. He would never admit that he didn't care enough about me to change, and he didn't care enough about me to fight for me.

Victor still had visitation rights to see me after I was placed into foster care. My birth father was the very typical image of tall, dark, and handsome. In photos I had of him, he was very tall, lean, and muscular. He had jet-black hair, dark eyes, and olive skin. He had a scruffy five o'clock shadow in the memories and pictures I had of him. I can understand why my birth mother was so attracted to him and why she was drawn in. He was a construction worker and was very good at what he did.

One night, I woke up suddenly. I would have been around three years old. My memories prior to that are quite hazy, likely because I was too young. That night I was in bed, gazing up at the ceiling. I rolled over on my mattress and caught glimpses of shadowy figures, all sleeping peacefully. I could tell my mom and dad were in their bed laying down.

I don't know much about what life was like in the care of my birth parents. I know from the social workers that there was abuse and neglect, and I am sure, among other things, drug abuse. One day, the social workers got a phone call because my birth mother's sister came over and found Olivea, my little sister, had been in her crib for hours and was drinking out of a spoiled bottle.

That wasn't enough reason for social services to take us away, but they were building a case. They had been involved in my birth mother's life since she had my oldest sister.

I had pictures of my birth father growing up in my Life Book. Victor looked unhappy in the pictures of him I had as a kid. As I got older, I realized he looked like he was high.

When I was an adult, I got a photo of me and my older brother from one of my sisters. She found it in the attic and brought it to me one day. I showed my mom the photo, and she just looked at the picture and said how heartbreaking it was because they probably took the photo in a visitation room at CSB. That was a big wake-up call for me.

I was in my early twenties and had my son. When I looked at him after giving birth, my heart felt like it had been shattered into a million pieces. I couldn't ever imagine leaving my child or doing something that would get my child taken from me. I can't fathom the feeling of my birth parents and I reuniting for a single hour and then having to part ways and continue living as if nothing had happened.

When my brother Damien finally told me about the day we were removed from our birth family, we were both adults. He came to my house one day to visit me and my kids, and we started talking about our childhood and reminiscing. Damien recounted that specifically and told me how Beverly took us all to CSB and then left without us. When Beverly left us, he cried, and I was so embarrassed that I hadn't asked him about the earlier events. Growing up, Damien was always there for me and protected me in every way he could, and it never occurred to me that maybe I should have been there for him as well.

He must have had so many emotions to work through, and he was left to do it on his own. When I realized he still remembered the day we were removed and the days after, I felt a pang of guilt for never having discussed it with him. I don't know why I grew up feeling like I couldn't talk to people about what we went through, even my own siblings. I wish I knew what made me and Damien think that we had to deal with our trauma in silence.

Damien told me that when the social worker took him to his first foster home, he cried for days. He told his foster parents he wanted his mom and cried when they told him he couldn't see her. He was only four years old when he went into foster care and when I found out that he had remembered all of it, my heart broke for him. After Damien left my house, I went into my room and tried to process everything he had told me. I felt an overwhelming sadness after talking to him and I didn't know how to deal with it. It wasn't my sadness to have. I think it made me realize that I had probably reacted the same way after being placed in foster care and my heart broke for the little girl that I once was.

It was hard to understand the feelings though, because I didn't have those memories. I had no recollection of Beverly leaving us at CSB or entering foster care. It felt impossible for me to imagine what I had been through. I felt the heavy weight of sadness on my shoulders and I couldn't seem to shake it, even though I had no recollection of the events.

There was another picture my sister had found. The photo was obviously from the early '90s, just by how everyone dressed. It was taken at Cedar Point, and it was my birth parents and another man and woman standing on either side of them. My birth dad had a cigarette hanging out of his mouth, wore a tie-dye tank top, and even had a black fanny pack around his waist. My birth mom was likewise in a '80s style shirt and had a bit of a belly that looked like she was pregnant. The picture was dated a few months after we were taken into custody and put into foster care.

I wrote letters to my birth mom as a teenager when I found out where she was and asked her what had happened that made Social Services take us all away. I found out many years later that she got all of my letters. She didn't know what to say, so she never answered them. When Victor finally got out of prison, he asked to see me. I told him it would be great to visit one day, but deep down inside, I didn't want to meet him. What do I say to someone who abandoned me? How could I ever look at this man and be okay, knowing I had to go through some dark traumas in my life because of his choices? *Where was he when I was moving from home to home? Where was my mom? How could they be okay leaving me like they did?*

One day, my birth father asked if he could visit me in Ohio for a couple of days. I felt a sense of dread and uncertainty creeping in. I had wanted to meet him in person for so long, but the thought of it happening filled me with panic.

After trying to avoid the situation at first, I finally mustered up the courage to reach out to him. I explained that I wasn't ready for his visit and that I needed more time to come to terms with everything. I suggested that maybe I could visit him in Minnesota when the time was right.

All that ran through my mind was, what if my parents were to find out I let him come visit, meet my kids, and let him in my home?

The idea of my birth father coming to my home, meeting my kids, and spending time with me was overwhelming. I couldn't shake off the fear that my parents might find out, especially given his criminal history, past drug addiction, and abusive behavior towards my birth mother. A memory of Victor picking up Damien by the neck and throwing him onto the couch surfaced in my mind. *Where did that memory come from? Did he abuse Damien like he did my mother?*

I had heard enough stories about him hitting my mom growing up and hitting us kids as well. I don't have any solid memories of it, but all of my other older siblings remembered. Reflecting on our conversations while he was in prison, I realized how naïve I had been to think that he cared about me. He was only reaching out to me because he had nothing better to do.

At the time, I felt safe and in control. I couldn't ignore the fact that his decisions led to me spending years in foster care and ultimately to his frequent incarcerations. It's a hard realization to accept, but one that I must confront if I'm ever going to move forward.

After I sent him the message, he messaged me repeatedly and told me he never did anything wrong. He called me at least twenty times within an hour and messaged me even more. I felt that maybe I had missed something. *How did I not pick up on this side of him before?* He had the nerve to pin all the blame on my birth mother and refused to take any accountability for his choices. Even though he had the opportunity to fight for custody of us, he chose to abandon us and run away. It was clear to everyone but him that he was guilty of neglecting his parental responsibilities.

Initially, I was fooled into accepting that he was not responsible for any of this. We avoided discussing the past, and I tried to move on from the pain he caused. He apologized for not being there for me when I was growing up, and I foolishly believed that was enough. I pretended that the terrible things he did never happened and tried to erase him from my memory. But as he sat there blaming everything on Beverly, I couldn't help but feel angry and betrayed. How could he be so callous and oblivious to the damage he caused? *How can he have the nerve to sit there and blame all of this on Beverly?*

I felt like the situation got out of control. After ignoring Victor, he must have reached out to his sister because later in the evening, I had a message on my phone from Victor's sister.

"I love you, Sheila. Seeing him being hurt is hard. I won't let him hurt you, but he doesn't even know how to deal with this."

I instantly responded, "In my opinion, he was being pushy for no reason. I don't mind talking to him, but him coming to Ohio is scary. What if I am having a bad day when he shows up? I talk to Victor on my good days, and I get to choose when. I went through six years of emotional and physical abuse, and I'll be damned if I let him tell me how I should feel and think. My parents spent the rest of my childhood repairing damage caused by him, so yeah, I don't have a lot of sympathy for him. He has hurt feelings?! I have a hurt soul."

When is this ever going to end? I keep getting myself pulled into shit like this with my birth family. I can't believe I let this go on for as long as I did. You knew this would happen, Sheila. You went through this entire thing with Beverly already and with Jamie and Laura. When are you going to learn?!!

I couldn't believe this conversation was happening. *I ended up in foster care for almost six years, bouncing from home to home, and his feelings were HURT! I spent all of my childhood not knowing who the hell I was or why the things that happened to me happened. He had the audacity to tell his sister his feelings were hurt and have her relay the message to me.*

I did have a hurt soul.

It was hurt back then as a little girl and still is hurt now as a grown woman. Nothing has changed.

Time didn't heal me and make it all better.

Through trial and error, I was able to find the best ways to cope with what I went through. It was my only option. When I was a young kid, I was required to face situations that even many mature adults are still having trouble dealing with. When I was hurt or afraid as a small child, I didn't have a mom or dad to turn to. I dealt with all of those emotions on my own, and I figured out how to survive. I found my own way out of the dark places with no help from anyone else. Most of the time, it was the families I was living with that hurt me, and I had to save myself.

I go through every day of my life with something creeping back up on me from my past that crushes me all over again. It can be a word, a voice, a smell, a sound, and things come flooding back, whether or not I want them to. I try to stay as busy as I can most days, so I don't give myself a chance to let the bad in. I usually go through a phase about once a year where everything hits me at once. After that, I go into a depression. Victor was never there when I needed a dad the most. Beverly was never there when I needed a mom the most.

I remember the last time I saw my birth mother, too. I remember the hurt; God, I remember the hurt. I saw her, but she couldn't see me. She was walking so close to me down the sidewalk, going somewhere. I don't know where she was going, but I realized where she had just come from.

I was six years old and living with a foster family. Our little sister, Emily, also lived with us. I didn't meet her until she came to live with this family, and by then, she was about a year old. When social services took us away, my birth mom, Beverly, was pregnant with another baby. I had already been in foster care for almost four years.

I am guessing they took her away for similar reasons that we were taken away. Still, I never asked.

We were in Toledo the day I saw my birth mom for the last time as a child. My foster mom, Karen, walked into Children's Services with my baby sister, Emily. I don't think I realized it that day, but my sister had to be there for a visitation. At that time, Beverly had already lost visitation rights to me and my older siblings. I don't remember having any visitations with Beverly, but I knew I did when I was little right after we were placed into foster care.

My foster grandma stayed in the van with me and Damien. I didn't know what was going on or why we were there, so we just sat in the van and I played with Damien while we waited. It felt like we had been in the van for a long time I got bored and started looking out the window, waiting for Karen to come back with Emily.

As I was looking out the van window, I noticed a woman walking out of the building. She looked familiar at first sight, and my heart started racing as I sat up straighter in the seat so I could get a better look. Once I was able to get a better look at her, everything slowed down. Even my heart felt like it had slowed down almost to where it was no longer beating.

I felt a wave of heat travel across my body as I realized it was *her*.

It was my mom! I knew it was, without a doubt. I recognized her face and her hair. She looked like the woman in my memories and in the pictures I had. I hadn't seen her in years, but I knew her face, and I knew without a doubt that it was my mom.

The sidewalk seemed so far away, even though we were parked parallel and right up against the sidewalk. Still, it was almost like the sidewalk wasn't even within reach.

It was cold out. My mom had a long brown coat on, and her hair looked how I remembered: blonde, curly, and right to her shoulders. I soaked in the image of her before my brain could process what was going on and what I should be doing. It hit me at once and I realized I was sitting there staring at her when I needed to be trying to get her attention.

I banged on the window with my hand and called out to her. I attempted to slide open the door, and it wouldn't budge. It dawned on me that my grandma had locked the doors. I remembered hearing the click as the doors locked right before I realized my mom was out there.

I turned to her. "Unlock the door, please!"

I kept banging on the window as I yelled out to my mom again and again. I frantically tried to slide the door open again, so I could escape and run to her, but it was still locked. My eyes stung as I blinked hard to push back tears. The tears were like a veil, obscuring my vision, but I refused to take my eyes away from my mom. I opened my mouth and screamed her name in desperation. I shouted as loud as I could, but my voice seemed to get swallowed up by the distance between us.

I brushed away the tears with the back of my hand, trying to clear my vision. Banging on the window, louder, I watched the back of Beverly as she walked further away. I was shaking in fear, dreading the possibility that she wouldn't notice me. I wanted her to rescue me.

My grandma's face was serious when she told me to take a backseat and be quiet. I screamed as loudly as I could one last time, praying she would hear me and turn around. *Please mom, see me! Please turn around! I need you. Please stop walking away!* Every beat of my heart seemed to echo in my ears, and I could feel the intensity of its rhythm as it pounded in my chest. I could barely hear my voice when I yelled out to her one last time.

I watched as Beverly finally turned the corner. She was gone. I tried to get her attention, but she was oblivious to the sound of my voice, and never even looked in my direction. *Please, come back… don't leave me here.*

Why didn't I fight harder? Why didn't I unlock the stupid door? It was too late, though. Just like that, she was gone, and I was broken all over again. I knew I would never see her again. I had a chance to fight my way out, and I couldn't do it. That was my chance to see my birth mom again, and tell her what I was living through. If she had only known, she would have rescued us and taken us from those people. But, I couldn't do anything. I was helpless. I blinked furiously to get the tears out of my eyes.

I hate her. I hate her so much. She knew Damien I were here, and she didn't care. She didn't even try to see us. I looked away from the empty sidewalk and covered my eyes with my hands. *I hate you!!*

Minutes later, Karen came walking out with my baby sister.

I told her what happened. She didn't care, though. She told me to calm down and sit back. I hated Karen for not caring about me and what I was feeling, but at that moment, I hated my mom so much more.

It still hurts me today to know I was so close to something different. What if I had gotten out of the van? What if I had just unlocked the door and ran after my mom? Would she have realized she was making a huge mistake? Would she have saved us?

I don't know, but I don't think it would have changed anything, and there was nothing that was going to make Beverly care more about her children than herself. Once Karen was back in the van and got my sister buckled in her car seat, I moved to the back row of the van where I normally sat. The entire ride home letting the pain I felt fuel my anger.

I will never, EVER, end up like my mother.

Sometimes that day comes back to haunt me. Sometimes, it feels so real, as if it happened all over again. I don't know what it is about me that makes me feel pain like that. My heart hurts thinking about that day and knowing what it felt like to lose my mother again. Back then, she was a fantasy, much like my birth father. But, of course, they were just fantasies, and I had so many scenarios for how I ended up where I was.

CHAPTER 7

During my time in foster care, I was shuffled between multiple families, some of which were so distant that the memories of them have become hazy. I struggled to recall their names, but their faces still lingered in my mind. However, one family, in particular, had a significant impact on my life and left an indelible mark on my memory.

I moved in with the Kessler's when I was six years old, and they became my foster family for almost two years. Their house was a magnificent white home, reminiscent of those you see in fancy subdivisions in rich neighborhoods.

It had two stories, large windows, and ample natural light. They also had a lake house on Round Lake in Michigan. We didn't live in the big, white house for very long. Soon after we moved in, they began building a new home in a small town in Northwest Ohio. During the time the house was being built, we lived in the lake house until the construction was complete.

They were best friends with a doctor, and the doctor and his family were building a house next door in the woods where the Kesslers were building their house. I remember Karen and Gary and their two boys the most out of the seven foster families I lived with because I had lived with them the longest, and I was finally old enough to remember things.

A couple of years ago, my husband and I separated for four months, and during that time, I moved back into my childhood home with my mom. My parents had divorced a few years prior and my mom stayed in the house I grew up in.

One day, while she was away, I became curious and searched through her bedside nightstands. It was then that I stumbled upon a notebook containing information about my siblings and me that social workers had provided to my adoptive parents when we were taken in. As I perused the notebook, my heart sank, and a sickening feeling crept into the pit of my stomach.

I always had a feeling in my mind that maybe everything was all just imagined. It turned out everything I remembered was accurate. The social workers knew about it and shared that information with my adoptive parents. My parents knew more than what they ever let on. They never talked about it or asked me about it, so I assumed they knew nothing. Growing up, I never talked much about what happened to me in foster care.

Occasionally, I would talk about minor details that didn't give away too much. I remember thinking as a kid that I shouldn't tell anyone what I went through. I knew the trauma I experienced messed with my head and my thoughts, and I was afraid that if I told anyone else that, it would somehow traumatize them by hearing any of my stories.

I sat on my mom's bed sobbing as I read through this notebook and re-lived things that were supposed to be forgotten long ago. *How could they have known about these things that happened and never say anything to us?*

They always loved us so much. Even if I didn't know it back then, I know it now. My brother and I were always causing trouble. We did anything from setting things on fire, breaking things, stealing, lying. I think we both thought we knew how our lives would end up, and at least if we did things to sabotage, then we were in control. We always had this genuine fear of our new family giving us back, even if we didn't do anything wrong. As children, we decided if they were going to give up on us, then we might as well give them reasons to.

Not long after we went to stay with what would eventually be our adoptive parents, my brother and I went to Vacation Bible School (VBS) at our church. In between activities, Damien went outside and slashed the tires on a bike of a girl who lived in our neighborhood.

Her parents found out and called the cops. We were all shocked when the police showed up to question me and my brother about what he had done earlier that day. Damien and I were both crying, and I was not sure what was going through his head, but I figured I knew how this was going to end. The police officer left after talking to us, and I turned and looked at Damien next to me on the couch. Seeing him cry made me cry even more. I was scared, but this wasn't the first time we had both been in this position. Angela and Jack sat down across from us and neither of them yelled.

Angela started talking, calmly but sternly. I knew she was upset, but I did not expect her to say what she did.

"We aren't giving up on you. We aren't giving you back. It does not matter what either of you do; we are always going to love you. You can keep going on the way you are now and make this harder on all of us, or you can quit fighting and realize that we are not going anywhere."

I started sobbing more as she spoke. *Why is she saying this?* I had never had anyone say anything like that to me before. Over eight years of my life had passed, and I had never heard an adult say they will love me no matter what I do. I had never heard an adult say they would never give up on me. I had never heard an adult tell me that I didn't need to keep fighting anymore. *Just yell at us and let us go. I don't know how to let someone love me.* As the tears fell, the knowledge that I was protected comforted me. I felt liberated to openly express my emotions without feeling the need to put on a facade. My brother cried next to me on the couch, and I looked at him again, and I could see in his face that he was lost. I was lost, too. I didn't know how, but I knew we needed to give this a chance.

They went above and beyond to make sure we knew how much they loved us. As much as I wanted to, I never fully believed them, though. I always lived like the bottom would drop out because it always did. People always made promises to me before, but none of them held true. So why should I believe these people?

Whenever I encountered something positive, it was often followed by something more difficult than I had gone through previously. Why does that always seem to happen in life? For once, can something be right and stay right?

I loved the picturesque view of the lake from the house I lived in with the Kessler's. Every day, we would head to the woods where the new house was being built, and I loved the feeling of the crisp air on my face and the sound of birds chirping all around us. My good memories were few and far between, but they were etched into my soul. Karen didn't want a boy, which was clear in how she treated Damien. She had two boys already. Aiden, the older of the two boys, was always very nice to me. The younger boy, Kyle, who I think was probably biologically their child, was not very nice. He was our age and didn't get along with either of us.

During the winter, Damien and I would stand by the heater on this apartment complex we would walk to for the school bus. I would breathe in the crisp, cold winter air as I stood with Damien by the heater on the apartment complex. Our breaths formed puffy clouds in front of our faces. We would exhale forcefully to make bigger clouds from our breath. Our noses and cheeks would be rosy red from the cold. The heater emitted a warm, comforting wave that enveloped us, and we huddled close together, our bodies bundled up in layers of winter gear.

The light from the street lamp illuminated our faces, and we smiled at each other as we talked and laughed. We made up silly games to pass the time. The anticipation of the school bus arrival mingled with the warmth of the heater made those moments more memorable. I cherished those mornings with my brother and felt close to him. I knew no matter what life gave us, we would be in it together. I imagine our relationship wouldn't have been much different if we had been twins. We were so similar in so many ways, and we got each other in ways no one else ever could.

One night, Karen put me to bed after she gave me a glass of warm milk with sugar in it as usual. She always did this for me before bed, and it was one thing she did that made me feel loved and cared for. She did it to help me sleep, and she shook out my pillow every night to shake the nightmares out of my pillow. I had bad dreams often, and she helped me believe I could shake bad dreams out of my pillow. It was silly, but it worked, and the nights she did that, there were no bad dreams.

Some kindnesses she showed me stuck with me for a long time. Maybe by then, kindness wasn't something I was very familiar with.

My older sister Jamie came to live with us, too. She was there for a while, and then my little sister came along too. Her name was Emily, and she was born after I went into foster care, so I had never met her before. She couldn't have been more than a year old because she didn't walk.

Karen started homeschooling after my sisters came to live with us. And by homeschooling, I mean she left us all home alone. She seemed to always go early in the day and not come back home until it was close to dinnertime.

This part of my life was so traumatizing for me because they gave me a baby when I was only six years old that I had to take care of.

I fed my sister, changed her diapers, burped her, played with her, and read her stories. At the age of six, I was a full-time stay-at-home mom. Reading began to consume my thoughts and take up a large portion of my time as I became increasingly obsessed with it. I learned to read, and then it was all I wanted to do. I read so many books to my baby sister every day and many nights too before I put her to bed.

I messed up quite a bit as well, though. There are so many things I regret doing. If only I had been more mature and had the necessary abilities to handle her. Although my older brother and sister were available to provide help, there were a lot of occasions where I was left to do everything by myself.

After my older sister left, Emily was still there, so it was just me again taking care of her. We called her Mary Martha back then, though, or M&M for short. I loved taking care of her. It gave me a purpose, and she loved me so much. It was not always easy, and I guess it shouldn't have been, considering my age.

I still have the image of the rug burns all over her body etched into my brain. I would have to drag her everywhere because I was too little, and she was too heavy for me to carry.

Our foster family was Catholic and must not have liked her name and decided to change it to Mary Martha, even though legally that was not her name. I never called my sister Emily once the whole time she lived with us. I only knew her as Mary Martha. They had everyone else call her by a name they picked out.

Sometimes, Damien and I would fight over Mary Martha, and one time we were in the basement fighting. I kept asking him to let her go so I could take her. She had been crying, and I was trying to take care of her, but us fighting over her made her cry even more. He was pulling her feet, and I was pulling her arms, trying to get her away from him.

Eventually, he gave up and walked away and let me have her. After he walked away, I turned her over onto her back, and she had rug burns all over her belly from us, pulling her back and forth across the carpet. I felt sick to my stomach seeing the red marks all over her. I picked her up and put her over my shoulder and shushed her to calm her down. She put her head into the nape of my neck, still crying, and wrapped her little arms around me. I sat there with her until I calmed her down, and then I started rocking back and forth, singing to her. She was always in a diaper, probably because I never would get around to dressing her. I realized I had messed up fighting over her with Damien. *I will be more careful with you from now on.*

She was like my daughter. She was mine; I cared for her, and I was her mom in every sense of the word. I loved her so much, and I know it would not have been any different for any other six-year-old girl with a baby sister, but we had something a little more. A lot of older siblings help with their younger siblings, but the way I cared for her caused me to connect with her like I was her mom and not just her sister.

I was ten years old when my little brother Michael was born. In the beginning, I was obsessed with him. I wanted to hold him non-stop and take care of him. When my mom had my little brother, she set many boundaries for me. I wasn't allowed to give him a bottle regularly. Occasionally, I could give him a bottle when she was sitting with me, so I knew I wasn't taking care of him on my own. She didn't let me change his diapers unless she was with me helping, and that was few and far between. I never put Michael to bed or rocked him to sleep when he was a baby.

My mom knew what I went through with my baby sister, and she was afraid that I would blur the line. She feared I could not separate myself and just be his sister. She wanted to make sure that even though there was a baby now, I never had to deal with adult things.

I had already been a mother before, and my mom knew that and did everything she could to ensure I was just his sister. Some days, I would get mad at her for not letting me do things for my baby brother, but she always explained why we needed to be careful. It made me livid sometimes because I loved Michael so much, and part of me wanted to take care of him on my own with no help from her or my dad.

As I was growing up, my mom would always tell the story to people about how, when my brother was crying after drinking a bottle, I helped teach her how to burp him. He wasn't very old and my mom was trying to burp him because he had just finished his bottle. She knew he needed to burp, but he could not get it out.

I saw what she was doing and suggested that she rub and push in an upward motion firmly on his back and then pat hard. She let me show her how to do it, and I put my hand low on Michael's back and put pressure on his back as I worked my way up, and then patted his back between his shoulder blades. She tried it then on her own, and after a couple of times, he finally let out an enormous burp and stopped crying.

Many years later, she confided to me that it was a bittersweet moment when I taught her how to burp her baby, as it made her heart heavy knowing why I had the experience to do so while I was only ten years old. She wasn't upset that I showed her or that she didn't know. It had taken her a while to understand that a large portion of my childhood had been devoted to being a mom myself. I knew everything about taking care of a baby when I had no business knowing any of that.

One day, when I was watching Mary Martha, I put her up on the counter in the kitchen. I went into the living room and retrieved a diaper to change her. My brother and sister and I were at home, and we got into an argument, which caused me to be sidetracked. The realization hit me that I left Mary Martha on the kitchen counter. I dashed around the corner of the living room. She was on her back, wiggling closer and closer to the edge of the counter and I could see it happening.

As I ran forward, I realized she was at the edge and about to fall off the counter.

I yelled out, "No!", but it was too late.

I heard her body hit the linoleum with a loud smack. I watched it happen in slow motion, mortified that she was wiggling off the edge of the countertop. After she hit the ground, there was complete silence for a moment, and then all at once she sucked air into her mouth, and the sound of her screaming came. I couldn't believe I had let that happen to her. She was my responsibility, and I failed her. *How could you let this happen, Sheila!!*

She screamed so loud. I have never been able to forget the blood-curdling cries coming from her that day. Anytime that memory comes back to me, I hear her little body smacking against the floor and remembering that sound still makes me feel sick to my stomach.

I picked her up in my arms, and I started crying as I bounced her in my arms and shushed her, trying to calm her down. *It's fine, it will be fine. I don't think anything is broken. I just need to calm her down and it will be okay.* Jamie and Damien tried to help calm her down too but, I took her back and started rocking her, and she finally calmed down.

Seeing that happen and knowing it was my fault stuck with me for the rest of my life. I knew I should have never been in that situation, and I thought that if we had been with my birth mom, then none of this would have happened. She would have been there taking care of her, and I never would have had to. I still had this fantasy about who she was.

I still sometimes wonder why I put Mary Martha on the counter. I saw Karen change her on the kitchen counter at times, and I must have thought it was okay. It was stupid.

The worst experience of my life was when my birth mother got custody of Emily back.

Our foster parents let us know one day that Beverly would be taking Emily back. My older sister had already left to go live with her biological father. It crushed Damien and me when they told us that Emily was leaving, and we were more crushed when we found out she was going back to our birth mother. *Why would anyone let Beverly take Emily back? Why is only Emily going back? Maybe this means that she is getting better and soon me and Damien will finally get to go back home.*

Still, it didn't make a lot of sense that if they were testing her to see if she could be a mom, that they give her a baby instead of her two older children. It would be harder taking care of Emily than me and my brother. We could take care of ourselves, so I thought it would have made more sense for us to go first and then Emily. I didn't want to be apart from Emily at all, though. I guess it didn't matter how it was going to happen as long as we ended up together again.

When Emily left, my entire world felt like someone had ripped apart it. I needed her at that time in my life. I needed something to care for to distract me from everything else. Emily needed me, too. Beverly wouldn't be able to take care of her as I did. I knew it was a mistake that they were doing this. How could they take my sister like that? How can people do that to children?

No one ever talked about me and my brother going back to my birth mom, and I got scared that maybe that would never happen. When Emily left our house, I sobbed, and I could barely catch my breath. I clung on to her before she left, holding her as tight as I could and giving her as many kisses as I could. I told her I loved her so much and that I would see her soon.

Just like that-she was gone out of my life. It left me with a piece of my heart missing. Beverly got Emily back, but she ripped her away from me. Emily was gone, and I did not know if I would ever see her again. All I could feel was the emptiness in my heart.

I waited for my mom to come back for me, to fight for me like she did for Emily.

She never came.

When I found out that she had signed off her rights to me and my brother, I felt like I had been abandoned all over again.

I found out later that Beverly signed off her rights to all of us, except for Emily. My brother and I belonged to the state after Emily left. The court made a deal with Beverly that if she signed off rights on the rest of the kids, they would give her a chance to start over with Emily.

Losing her destroyed me, but it hurt just as much that my mom didn't try to see me or fight for me.

She took Emily, but it had been years since the last visitation I had with her. Was I nothing to her? The day I found out that she had signed us over to the state, I made two decisions.

One, I was going to be a mother one day and have a lot of kids, and I would take care of them in the way my mother never could.

Two, I was going to do something great with my life, and I was going to make her regret giving up on me.

The Kessler's never liked Damien. Gary might have liked him to an extent, but he was rarely there, so he never spent any amount of time with either of us. Karen was kind to her two sons, but the tone in her voice when she spoke to Damien made it obvious that she hated him. She always spoke to him in a stern or angry voice, and she never smiled when she talked to Damien.

Anytime our foster brothers did something wrong, they were rarely disciplined, and if Damien did something wrong, he was disciplined harshly. Karen seemed to yell at him constantly, and she would grab his arm tightly when she yelled at him or get close to his face like she wanted to make sure he felt scared. She was not always extremely kind to me, but I did not get disciplined or yelled at in the same way my brother did, and I felt guilty about that, especially when we were both doing something wrong.

From the beginning of our stay with them, Damien often would sneak food during the day and even more at night. He was a lanky seven-year-old with endless energy. Damien was always hungry, and he never gained any weight, so I knew they didn't prevent him from snacking because they were worried about his weight. They also had a lot of money, from what I could tell, because they had a beautiful lake house and were building an even larger house.

He never talked to me about why he snuck food when he wasn't supposed to, but back then, I thought it was normal that we only ate at meals or when our foster parents gave us permission. To him, it probably did not seem like that big of a deal to take food. He figured out that if he asked for food, they would say no, so he started doing it when they weren't watching.

I knew by then, after all the families we lived with, that every family had different rules, and we had to adjust quickly or there would be consequences. It didn't matter if the last family was not so strict about eating snacks, it only mattered that this family had rules, and there was no leniency to them. Fear of the repercussions kept me from straying from the rules and made me conform to them faster.

I had lived with enough families to know that even if someone seems to be safe, at any moment they can change and decide to do something that could hurt me. I didn't always follow the rules, but I noted the things that would make my foster parents snap and I made sure to not do those things.

This ended up being something that shaped the entire relationship we had with Karen and Gary. Each time Damien got caught taking food, the punishments would get worse. In the beginning, it started with just yelling, and Damien started to yell back. Sometimes, he would start to hit and kick if they got too close to him or grabbed him aggressively.

One day, Karen was restraining him because they had been fighting. Damien started fighting back. Watching Damien being restrained was a common thing after we moved in with the Kessler's.

A social worker had come to the house one day and taught Karen restraint methods to use on Damien when he got out of control. He had a lot of anger issues, and I know it was not good when he hit or kicked, but he was so little. I didn't understand why they needed to restrain him at all.

That day, things escalated when Damien and Karen were fighting, and she got on top of him while he was lying face down on the floor. He was fighting to get out from underneath her and screaming. She put his hands behind his back and held them there with one hand. Then, she held his head down with her other hand and she straddled him. Seeing him cry and hearing him screaming out that it hurt made me panic. *Just stop! Quit hurting him!* I knew I needed to get her away from him, but nothing came to mind.

My brother was still yelling and fighting, trying to get her off him. I didn't know what to do, but I got an idea that I might find something in the van. I ran to the van parked outside across the street in front of the garage to see if I could find something. Searching through the van, I came across a safety pin in the cup holder and grabbed it before running back inside. I got on Karen's back and wrapped my arms around her to hold her, and I started stabbing at her hand that was holding his hands behind his back.

Karen yelled out, and I could tell I had hurt her. Pushing me off of her back, she yelled, "Get back, Sheila!" She got off of Damien, dragged him to his room, and shut the door before she yelled at me for getting involved and stabbing her with the safety pin. I wasn't sorry that I did it, and I was still furious that she had been hurting Damien.

I hated the way she treated him, and I felt so helpless. I wish I could have done more to help him. They never treated me as badly as they treated him, and I could never understand why. He was just a little boy. He never once did anything to me. We sometimes fought like brothers and sisters, but he always cared for me and protected me. He wasn't bad; he just didn't listen all the time. What was so bad about that? He made bad choices sometimes, but Karen always handled it so aggressively.

Sometimes they would have Damien locked in his room all day and not let him eat anything or come out. Damien would get enraged with them when they put him in his room, and he would try to fight them. He was only seven, though. He couldn't have done much harm to them. His fighting turned into threats. The only thing he knew how to do was fight, and that was what he did.

They started propping a chair against his door under the doorknob at night before they went to bed, so he wouldn't be able to get out.

If he got out, they would hear the chair fall. I heard Gary and Karen talking about it, so I knew why they had the chair blocking the door.

Eventually, propping a chair on the door wasn't enough and they made Damien sleep in leg braces at night to prevent him from being able to get out of bed to get food or do anything else. The first time I saw him lying in bed with leg braces on, I wanted to scream.

I wanted to hurt Gary and Karen for doing this to my brother.

At night, after everyone else was asleep, I would get up and grab food for Damien. Tiptoeing into the kitchen, I would try to be as silent as I could, gathering whatever food I could find that Damien could eat. I tiptoed down the hall from the kitchen to his room and eased the chair out of the way. I opened the door and walked in and gave Damien the food so he could eat.

One night, I grabbed some food from the kitchen and walked carefully to his bedroom. Moving the chair aside, I opened the door and then squatted down. I had been in trouble already for getting caught sneaking him food and I didn't want to go all the way in his room in case someone heard me. I was going to drop the food inside the door and whisper to Damien, so he knew there was food there.

When I opened the door and looked in, Damien was already on the floor. I jumped back a little, scared, because I didn't expect to see him out of bed. He was on his stomach, using his elbows and forearms to drag himself across the carpet. The leg braces prevented him from being able to walk at all since they buckled around his feet, and there was a bar that ran between the two shoes that made it impossible for him to take a step.

I pushed the food inside as Damien looked up at me, and I whispered to him, "I brought you food."

He pulled himself closer to the door and whispered back, "Thank you."

"I have to go to bed before someone hears me."

"Okay," he responded.

I hesitantly shut the door quietly, and I felt so guilty that I was leaving him in there like that, but I knew it would only make it worse if I tried to do anything else.

After I was adopted, I found out that Gary and Karen told the social workers that they locked him in his room and used the leg braces because they were afraid he would kill them.

We had some good times with this family, though. It made the bad times harder because it wasn't always a nightmare. It made it harder to know how to feel because some days were good, but then there was so much bad too. I learned to swim and fish during our first summer there, and during our first winter I learned to ice skate. Even in winter, we took advantage of being out on the lake as much as possible. We had a lot of fun, and something was always happening, especially during the summer. We would always ride our bikes up and down the street, since there was hardly any traffic.

Before living with the Kesslers, my siblings and I stayed with another foster family for a short period - maybe weeks, maybe months. Their house was beautiful and had a fenced-in backyard with a playhouse and swings. I was with my brother and older sister when I lived with this family. I remember spending most of our time outside during the summer, enjoying the warm weather, and playing with the other kids that lived there.

One day, as the warm sun beat down on us, we played in the playground area, pretending to be Power Rangers with our foster siblings. My sister, Jamie, had claimed the role of the Pink Ranger, but I desperately wanted a turn. I begged her to let me be the Pink Ranger just this one time, but she refused, saying that I wasn't good enough to be the Pink Ranger. Frustrated and angry, I stomped off towards the house where our foster mom was making lunch. I stormed through the back door and saw my foster mom standing at the wooden cutting block slicing up cheese with a knife.

"Jamie won't let me be the Pink Ranger again," I whined.

She slammed down the knife and turned toward me, her eyes filled with anger. I was shocked at how upset she got. She turned from the cutting block where she was making lunch and yelled at me.

"I am fed up with your tattling!"

She went into a kitchen drawer next to where she was standing and grabbed a roll of duct tape out of it. I didn't understand why she grabbed the tape, but I felt I was in a lot of trouble because of how tense her body was, and the look on her face that gave away that she was furious.

She ripped a piece off and duct taped my mouth shut. She told me if I was going to keep tattling, then I was going to have to keep the duct tape over my mouth until I learned my lesson. I didn't fight back and didn't try to take the tape off. I was worried I would be in trouble if I did.

"Get back outside right now."

Carefully and without making a sound, I turned my body and left through the back door. I settled down at the picnic table, the back door creaking shut behind me. I was so humiliated that I couldn't bring myself to go near the playground and silently hoped that none of the children would spot the tape on my lips.

I watched the other kids playing, and I started crying sitting there. *I shouldn't have gone inside. If I had just stayed outside, none of this would have happened. If my sister wasn't such a brat and always had to have her way, none of this would have happened.* I blamed myself; I blamed my sister, and I blamed everyone for this. *Why couldn't I keep my mouth shut about anything?*

After a while, my foster mom brought lunch out for everyone except me, and all the kids sat around me at the picnic table.

Jamie sat down next to me. "Why do you have tape on your mouth?"

I couldn't respond, and I think she knew better than to press the issue. As I looked down, I could feel the heat of embarrassment covering my skin, turning it a deep shade of red. I never took the tape off my mouth to ask if it was okay for me to eat lunch. I felt completely humiliated and embarrassed as I sat there watching the other kids eat. None of the other kids said anything else to me. They all knew it was better to stay out of it and let me sit out my punishment in silence.

In those moments, sitting there with the duct tape on my mouth, I felt like I had messed up. I played the day back through my head, trying to remember how many times I tattled on my sister or brother. It had always been apparent to me that I struggle with being able to control how much I talk and having the knowledge of when to keep quiet. I knew I did tattle sometimes, but I always felt that I had a good reason.

Even though I didn't quite understand what was happening, I knew then that it was not a good thing to tell adults things. I decided that day I would try to be better and not tattle on anyone anymore because I never wanted to have to sit there with that embarrassment again.

After the other kids ate, they got up and went back to playing their game. I sat out there for what seemed like a couple of hours before my foster mom came out and told me she would take the duct tape off if I could stop tattling. I nodded, and she pulled the tape off. My skin felt raw from having the tape cling to my skin for so long. She never offered me lunch, and I figured it was probably too late to eat at that point. I walked out to where my other siblings were and started playing again, trying to put the incident out of my head.

CHAPTER 8

I could describe my story to you in countless ways, from every angle and perspective imaginable, but I fear it would still fall short of conveying the raw, overwhelming pain that had been my constant companion.

Some days, my heart beats so frantically in my chest that I fear it will burst from the weight of my grief. It's a suffocating sensation, as if the weight of the world is pressing down on me and I can't draw a breath.

There are days, every word, every hurt, every memory comes back, and as much as I wish it away, it stays, lingers inside of me, waiting… waiting… waiting for me to break.

I always did.

I am telling this story now because I need to get these things out of my head, or they will haunt me forever. Each day I write, I find more and more liberation. These were some of the darkest days of my life. They were the most trying days on my soul.

Sometimes, I wonder if I truly survived those early years, or if I am simply existing, day by day, in a state of limbo. But despite the constant battles that I fight with my past, I refuse to let it define me any longer.

For so long, I felt like I was silenced. I was afraid to speak, afraid to be seen or heard. As a child, I did not know how to deal with that, so I shrunk myself. I made myself small. During my years in foster care, I felt like I was drowning. I couldn't open my mouth and cry out for help. I had to keep fighting and swimming toward the surface. The sun was there, showing me the way to the surface, so I could break free, and finally breathe again, but I was so tired of fighting, and I didn't know if I would ever break through the surface. If I could just keep moving and pushing forward, then I would have to reach the surface, eventually. If I stayed still, I would fall further down and most certainly die.

I couldn't let that happen.

I deserved better than that.

One day, I would reach the surface, and I would break free. I would be able to take a breath and have the ability to speak again. I would break my silence one day. It was just a matter of when.

I was removed from my family at three years old because of neglect, sexual abuse, drug abuse, physical abuse, domestic violence, and probably other things. I went days and weeks eating chicken noodle soup and peanut butter and jelly for every meal because my parents spent all the money they had on drugs. We were deprived of cleanliness, nurturing, and love.

When my parents were high on drugs, they didn't go out of their way to pick us up and tell us they loved us. That wasn't *our* life.

That wasn't *our* normal.

We suffered in so many ways and continued to suffer even after we were gone from them. Why does God give us these trials? Are they trials? Why do I feel like all of my life has been a trial to see if I could handle a little more, a little more, a little more? When does it end? Does it end when I finally break? Will this ever end?

Every time I think I have moved on, I still find myself coming back. Every time I believe I have made it out, I realize maybe I haven't. I still long for my parents. Nothing in my life was ever how it was supposed to be.

I mourned people who were still alive because that was all I could do. I mourned the life that I lost and the parents I lost even though I did not know what that life even was.

I wished for a mom and dad while in foster care. Every time I saw the first star come out at night, the most prominent and brightest star, I always looked for it and made a wish. Every time I prayed, I asked for a mom and dad.

At three years old, I take note of my daughter's personality and the amount of love and care she needs to grow properly. I didn't have a fraction of that. It is my hope that she will know the kind of love that I never had the chance to experience. I love wrapping my arms around her and hearing her soft voice as she talks to me about random things. As I look into her blue eyes, I can feel the love she has for me as I gently wind one of her curls around my finger. I have given her a different kind of love because I know what it was like to never have it. I am stern with her and strict when I need to be, but always tell her I love her and show her I love her through my actions as her mother.

I hold her face between my two hands and tell her how beautiful she is, how strong she is, and how brave she is. Each and every day I take the opportunity to build her up and I have no intention of stopping. I never, ever want her to feel the pain in her heart that I have, and I hope I can help protect her from those things.

In the quiet of the night, I could be the person I wanted to be. I had the perfect family, the perfect life. Nothing could pull me away from that. Then, the sun would rise again, and I would wake up to what was my reality. Never knowing what would happen. Living in constant fear. It was the emotional pain that hurt me the most.

I was unloved, unseen, unwanted… knowing these things and feeling that would be what broke me if ever I did break at all.

I had been given back to social services so many times already that I thought my heart would physically break if someone else gave me back. For so many years, I thought that love was beyond my reach. I was damaged, used goods. Who could ever want me? My own parents didn't want me.

I wondered often where they were and if they thought about me, but as I got older, I knew they didn't. I used to think the

Kessler's wanted me. Sometimes I felt like they did. On other days, I could tell they hated me. I had lost hope for so long already. I had been in foster care for four years already and had lived with five foster families. Each time I went to another home, I packed my things in a garbage bag, and I left what memories I could behind me. I started to give up hope, though, and each year in foster care, I started realizing that there was a chance that I might never get out.

There was no end in sight and that was the most execrable part.

The unknown.

One night, around 11:00 p.m., Karen, our foster mom, dropped my brother and me off at CSB in Toledo. She walked up to the window inside the building on the first floor. A receptionist worked there, and I was shocked to see someone inside so late. I had been in this building countless times, but never this late at night. It was empty and eerie. There was no one else around that I could see, and the lights were very dim in the front foyer area.

I wondered how many children had been dropped off in the middle of the night because the adults couldn't take it anymore. I was sure it happened often.

Karen told the receptionist something, but I could not hear what she was saying. Damien and I were standing by the wall waiting, and we were not sure what was going to happen. I was tired and wanted so badly to go to sleep. I heard the receptionist tell Karen that she could not take me back with her. She told her that if Damien stayed, then I stayed too.

We were not getting split up.

It made me heartbroken at that moment because I realized what was happening. She was going to try to leave my brother here and take me back with her. She tried to take me with her, but the receptionist refused to let her walk out with me. I could tell Karen was furious when she turned toward us, and then she turned to the door and walked out of our lives forever. She left us with nothing but the clothes on our backs, no clothes that had been bought over the last two years, no birthday presents, no Christmas presents, no toys, and no pictures. We didn't have our Life Books with us either.

We were six and seven years old.

She didn't even say goodbye to us.

My social worker showed up only a short time after and took us to her office, so we could sleep, and we slept on her floor until morning.

The next day, our social worker, Aunt Sarah, took us shopping to buy us some clothes. She bought me a bright pink sweatshirt with Tweety Bird that said in big giant letters; *I Was Born Lucky*. I loved that shirt and I wore it for years, all the way through middle school. It was my favorite shirt because she bought it for me, but more so because I felt like she picked out because of what it said.

My social worker returned to the Kessler's and retrieved the things we had gone to their house with, including our Life Books and pictures. Karen had no intention of ever giving us back our stuff, and she tried to keep all of our stuff even after Sarah was there to pick it all up. We were helpless, in need of a home and love, and no one could provide that for us.

After the night Karen dropped us off, I started asking Aunt Sarah to adopt us. Every time I saw her, I begged her to adopt us, but she said she couldn't. I knew Sarah would have made the best mom in the world. If I could just convince her that Damien and I were a perfect fit for her, then she would change her mind.

She was our only constant. She was always there to put our pieces back in place and help us move on. I wish I had been more honest with her growing up.

By that time, several social workers knew us by name and would stop in Aunt Sarah's office whenever we came in. That place was like our second home, most familiar to us because that is where we always ended back up. In many ways, Sarah was all I knew as a mother. She gave me an idea of what an actual mother would be like, and I clung on to that for years. After the first couple of years in foster care, I cried more because I missed Sarah than my own parents.

After another couple of years of living in multiple other foster homes, I finally went and lived with a woman I called Grandma Jo. She lived in a trailer park in Toledo, and I think she was related to the people I lived with before. That's how I thought I ended up with her. I remember her always being around when I lived with the family before her, and after I went to live with Grandma Jo, the other family would come over often.

Grandma Jo is best described as a grumpy, cranky old woman. I hated coming home from school even more than normal when I lived with her. There wasn't much to do at Grandma Jo's and I usually ended up doing something that got me into trouble. It got to where I knew I would do something to get yelled at or punished, so I dreaded having to be home with her.

Despite being potty trained before going into foster care, I started having accidents because of a fear of using the bathroom. When I moved in with Grandma Jo, I didn't realize she had a strict "no-accident" policy. Not that any of my other foster families were okay with me having accidents. The punishments were just harsher with Grandma Jo.

She constantly smacked me in the face and upside the head when I had accidents. I had lived with her for months, and one day she found out I had an accident, and she took me into the bathroom as she screamed at me. She was yelling something at me, and I was standing in the bathroom looking in the mirror. I could tell I was about to cry. Grandma Jo smacked me so hard across the face that it instantly brought me to tears. I held my face and looked at her, shocked, but she had no remorse in her face. She yelled at me to get cleaned up and slammed the door behind her as she walked out of the bathroom.

She didn't understand how embarrassed I was to go to the bathroom in a house with strangers. I wasn't doing this to upset her, and I wished I knew how I could stop doing it. Every time I had an accident, I hated myself more. I could not stop them, though. I told myself I was going to stop so I wouldn't get in trouble anymore, but they kept happening.

Grandma Jo never asked why I had accidents. She didn't care; she wanted me to stop.

I am guessing at some point, maybe someone shamed me or made me feel embarrassed, or it came from the fact that I was always living with strangers. Being a girl, I was mortified, especially by boys or men being in the house when I had to go to the bathroom. And eventually, it was just anyone.

Grandma Jo and I would always take long walks around the trailer park in the evening, and I enjoyed those walks, being able to get out of the house. She didn't have anything for me to do in the house, anyway. So, those walks were fun. She would usually talk to me about whatever recent gossip she heard, and I would walk and listen. Even if I had been in trouble earlier in the day, we did the walks every evening, and she would mostly do the talking, but sometimes I would talk about things, too.

She had a boyfriend who lived in the trailer park, and she invited him over for dinner one night. She made meatloaf and mashed potatoes, one of my least favorite foods. It must have been terrible because I vomited it up at the dinner table in front of them.

I thought maybe I threw up because I was sick. I didn't just spit it out. Grandma Jo took me into the bathroom, slapped me across the face, and told me I embarrassed her in front of her friend. Then she walked out and left me in the bathroom to cry alone. She was a mean, old, and bitter lady.

I imagine at her age she had raised her own kids and probably did a lot with her grandkids. Some of them would come over from time to time. I am clueless as to why I was ever put in her care, and I can't comprehend why she wanted to foster kids. She clearly did not like kids at all. I didn't understand why people who don't like kids decide to become foster parents.

My social worker would come to pick me up now and then, and I would have visitations with my brother. They couldn't keep us together for some reason. My brother ended up with a terrific family, though. They were nice to him. I only saw them on a few occasions, but I loved them like family because they loved my brother like family. I loved our visitation days, though my brother was getting to that age where I was just the annoying little sister. But I suppose it was bound to happen at some point.

After about six months or so living with Grandma Jo, we ended up being on the news for a program called "Home for Keeps." It was a segment done once a month by a news anchor for a local news channel. This program featured children in foster care and aimed to help them find permanent homes by sharing their stories with the public. Our social worker picked us up one day and took us to Krispy Kreme in Toledo, where we were interviewed by a beautiful, tall news anchor with striking blonde hair. As we learned how to make donuts, she asked us about our favorite things and individual interests.

In my one-on-one interview, she asked me a couple of questions before she asked me what my favorite food was.

I answered in a baby voice, "mack-in-cheese."

She stopped the cameras, got down on my level, and looked me right in the eye. She told me that this was not a joke, and that I needed to answer the questions seriously because someone might want to adopt me.

I didn't realize how serious that was, and I felt terrible after the fact that I treated it like a joke. *Why can't you ever just be serious, Sheila? I can't believe I just got myself yelled at. I need to take this seriously if I ever want to find a family and get away from Grandma Jo.*

I finished the interview and tried to do my best and act mature during the rest of our time there. The best part was all the donuts we got to eat. We got a free shirt and hat as well, and I wore them both home. I went home and was filled with excitement at the thought of being on t.v. I felt so special that I was able to get to do something so cool.

A couple of months later, Sarah came to visit me at Grandma Jo's house. Sarah walked into the house, holding a letter and a photo album. My heart pounded with anticipation. She sat down beside me on the couch and handed me the letter. My eyes scanned the page, and my heart leaped as I read the words:

it was a couple introducing themselves and saying they wanted to meet me and Damien because they wanted to adopt us.

Not foster….adopt!

My eyes widened as I read the letter again, and I couldn't help but smile. I looked up at Sarah with complete happiness, and then she handed me the photo album and looked through each page with me. The couple took pictures of their home and every person in their family. They put them all in that binder, so Damien and I would know more about them before we met them. I could have looked at each one of those photos for hours, soaking up each face and creating the image of the life that might be mine. I didn't have a lot of time though, because Sarah had to leave to visit Damien, and she had to take the photos with her.

This can't really be happening! I can't believe these people want to meet me!

For the past six years, I had never dared to dream of a forever home. I always assumed that I would eventually return to my birth parents, but that dream had long since faded. The thought of being adopted was surreal. Part of me yearned for a family of my own, but another part of me still longed to see my birth parents again, despite everything that had happened. My mind raced with conflicting emotions, and I didn't know what to do.

CHAPTER 9

I believed God was listening to my prayers all those years since I first started praying at four years old. I didn't know it then, but I would soon find out that God maybe had a plan for me after all.

This is that part of my story.

It really isn't my story at all, though.

Jack and Angela were from two tiny towns that weren't even considered towns at all. Angela worked at her parents' ice cream shop in Grand Rapids, Ohio. Jack lived in Grand Rapids and worked in the small town after high school. Jack would often stop by for a burger on his lunch breaks. Every time he visited, he would flash her a warm smile and try to engage her in conversation. Angela blushed, giggled, and tried to focus on her work. But she couldn't deny that she looked forward to his visits.

Eventually, Jack summoned the courage to ask Angela on a date.

Angela was in her junior year of college when they began dating. She lived off-campus in an apartment with two roommates. During Angela's last year of college, they moved in together in the apartment above where her parents lived in Delta, Ohio. Angela went to school for social work, and when she finished, she was hired as a social worker in Fulton County. Jack had owned his own gas station in the small town he grew up in, but one day he quit that job and started working at Lyden Oil Company.

They eventually married. Jack and Angela's wedding day was a joyous occasion, filled with laughter, music, and dancing. As they exchanged their vows, they both knew that they wanted to start a family together soon.

They wanted kids, so they actively started trying to conceive. But as time passed, their dreams faded. Each pregnancy ended in heartbreak, leaving them both feeling empty and hopeless. Angela's body seemed to betray her at every turn, and they both felt powerless to change their circumstances.

They clung to each other, praying and hoping for a miracle. Weeks turned into months, and months turned into years, but still they held onto their faith.

Finally, the day came when they received the news that no one ever wants to hear. Angela could never carry a child to full term. They both felt like their hearts had been shattered into a million pieces.

They kept praying and hoping for something to happen so they could have children one day. They were both so ready to start a family and raise their own kids, but they were at a loss because they were being robbed of the only thing they had ever wanted.

During those years, God wasn't just listening to my prayers; he was listening to their prayers too.

Angela and Jack decided to take classes so they could be licensed to adopt. The process for them to be licensed took months, but they got through it and they both got excited about the thought of adopting even though they still struggled with the fact that they would not be able to have children of their own.

During classes, the social workers often showed videos and pictures of children who needed families. One day during one class, the social worker doing the training showed a video of a girl and a boy who were eight and nine years old. When Angela and Jack saw the little boy and girl, something triggered inside them. They both felt a gravitational pull toward the kids they had not felt before.

A couple of days later, Jack's dad called and told Jack he had seen a little boy and girl on the news on a segment called "Home for Keeps," and he had recorded it and showed it to Angela and Jack. Ironically, it was the same two kids they had seen before during their classes.

God took not one, but two tragedies and somehow merged them in a way I could have never dreamed possible. God worked on a plan for me when I was at the worst times of my life. It did not come with no significant loss. Someone had to lose something for me to gain something. What would my life have been if they had never had those miscarriages? I wouldn't have my son or my daughter. I would have never met my husband. Everything had to work out precisely the way it did at exactly the time that it did. There are no accidents, there are no coincidences, and there is no chance.

Our lives were already laid out before God breathes life into our lungs. I believe that with all of my heart. Every time I think about how thankful I am for what happened, I feel like such a selfish person for thanking God when I know the tragedies Angela and Jack had before they met me. My heart aches, and I feel the tears pool in my eyes at just the glimpse of the thought that they could have had a child and carried it to term. The story I had would have been completely different if that had happened.

I wouldn't have lived the life I lived. Everything in my life was pointing to nothing and going nowhere.

When I finally accepted my fate and thought it was over for me, God showed me what he had been working on.

The first picture I saw of them was when my social worker brought the album to Grandma Jo's and showed me. In the picture, Angela and Jack were standing side by side, and Jack had his arm around Angela. You could tell by the look on his face he had been trying not to laugh. I saw happiness, genuine happiness. I fell in love with their faces at that moment. It had been so long since I met people with happiness that radiated from them.

I was floating on clouds. I started imagining this life for myself.

They were from a town I had never heard of, and everything seemed like a fairy tale to me. After I looked through the photo album, Sarah said they wanted to meet us, and that Damien and I could pick the place. After she left Grandma Jo's house, she went to visit Damien to show him everything. I hadn't seen Damien yet, but I was hoping he would be excited to meet them, too. At the next visitation, Damien and I had, we talked about the plans for when we would meet our potential family. Damien didn't care where we met them, and he told me I could choose the place.

I chose Taco Bell, which was my favorite fast-food restaurant. I was so excited to go and finally meet Angie and Jack. About a week later, two of our social workers drove us to Taco Bell to meet them.

I walked in and saw Angie and Jack sitting at a table. My heart was racing from the excitement. I was nervous, but I was so excited to finally see them in person for the first time. Seeing them sitting there made everything feel real.

For me, it was love at first sight.

They both turned toward us when we walked in the door, and their eyes were completely lit up with excitement. They both had the most genuine smiles I had ever seen before in my life. I looked into both of their eyes, and could have cried seeing how happy they were to see me. They had this look like I was a long-lost friend they couldn't wait to see again. It was confusing at first, because I never had a foster parent look so excited when I first met them, and in most cases I never saw them look that happy at all. Angie and Jack made me and Damien feel like we were the only two people that mattered in the world when they stood up to introduce themselves.

They were calm, as if trying to hide their excitement, but I could tell by their smiles and the ways their eyes lit up they were just as excited as I was.

They walked with us up to the counter to order food. I immediately started talking about random things. I was nervous, and I wanted them to like me, so I acted as bubbly and happy as I could. Damien and I both made jokes and tried to say things to get them to laugh. We got our food, and all of us sat down together to eat. Everything felt light and natural. I didn't feel any pressure, and it didn't take much time for me to be comfortable enough to act like my normal self. I was worried that they would not like how talkative I was, but I could tell that they didn't mind at all, so I kept talking. It had been so long since I could be myself around adults without any fear.

Angie and Jack laughed at all of our jokes and they joked around with us as well, trying to make me and Damien laugh. It worked, because I thought they were both so funny and could tell they both didn't take anything too seriously and like to have fun and act silly.

The meeting went exactly as we had hoped and turned out perfectly. Damien and I left Taco Bell feeling completely sure that they would want to see us again. I found out later that Jack and Angie felt the same way. After meeting us, they knew without a doubt that they wanted to adopt us. When I heard we would be moving in with Jack and Angie, I was the happiest I had been in years. I was filled with anticipation for the next chapter of my life, the chance to finally be a part of a real, loving family.

After months of preparation, the day had finally arrived to move in with Angela and Jack and give living together a try to determine if we would all be compatible. Angie and Jack came to Grandma Jo's house to take me to my new home, and I knew it could be my last time seeing Grandma Jo.

I found myself crying as I said goodbye to her. Saying goodbye to her left me with a unique feeling of sorrow that I had not experienced before. I felt immense hatred towards Grandma Jo, but maybe there were things I would miss.

Why was I so unhappy to leave her?

I tightly embraced her and felt the warmth of her body in my arms as I held on for a moment, soaking it all in. *I will miss you, but I am so glad that I am leaving.*

Perhaps I was just scared because she was familiar; now, I had to start over again. I had lived with seven foster families, and the idea of settling down scared me. How could I live a normal life after everything I went through in the last six years?

I was used to the unknown, the chaos, and the constant change. Could I settle down and be in one place? Could I let them love me, knowing they aren't my parents? Would I be able to love them? I still had this hole in my heart that my birth parents left.

We got in the car, left, and drove from downtown Toledo to Delta, this unfamiliar land, this scary new place I would hopefully build my life in. When you have lived most of your life in Toledo, even at a young age like I was, you notice when things are different in other towns. The houses were prettier;

the people dressed better, and everyone seemed happy, smiled, and knew each other. In big cities, it is so easy to be distant from people. I knew I liked this new town, though. I was so happy to be there.

Jack pulled into the drive, and there were two brand new bikes Angela's sister had bought for us as a welcome home gift. My eyes lit up when I saw them. It was the first time I had gone to a new family, and a gift was waiting for me. *I am so lucky!* We checked out our new bikes and then walked inside.

I looked around at the living room and then set my garbage bag with all of my things down on the floor next to me. I felt this weight lifted as I looked around and took my time noticing everything about the living room. *This house is perfect. I can see myself living here.*

I spotted a cat sitting on a recliner in the living room, and I walked right to it. I picked up this big white fluffy cat and held him in my arms as I turned to look at Damien. "Damien, look, they have a cat!" I was grinning from ear to ear. "His name is Boo-Boo Kitty," Angie said, smiling back at me. Damien didn't look very impressed, and he walked away to inspect the rest of the home. I put the cat down and followed.

Angie and Jack let us take our time checking everything out and then finally took us upstairs to see our bedrooms. There were three bedrooms upstairs, and Damien and I each got a room of our own. The rooms were ready and waiting for us when we arrived. They had arranged everything perfectly. There were beds with nice bedding, dressers, end tables, toy boxes that already had toys in them. There were clothes in the dressers already, which was surprising. In my bedroom, there was a mesh canopy attached in the corner of two walls, and it was overflowing with stuffed animals. Angie and Jack told us both that everything in the rooms was ours to keep. I wanted to cry hearing that, but my excitement overpowered all of my other emotions.

In the first couple of weeks, we were all in the honeymoon phase.

Everything was perfect.

Angie and Jack spent a lot of time getting to know us over the first few weeks. We went over the rules of the house, and it wasn't anything like the rules I had heard before. I realized I would have more freedom here. Damien and I spent a lot of time playing together, and I was so happy to be back with my brother. I loved him so much, and I was so happy he was there with me again. It wouldn't have been the same without him. The first couple of weeks were filled with playing and laughing. I was the happiest I had been in a really long time.

After a few weeks, the honeymoon phase came to an end. Damien and I were so used to not having stability. We didn't know what to do with it. Our routine was the same every day, and it made me feel uncomfortable. I hadn't been yelled at or hit in weeks. We woke up every day and did the same thing; we had breakfast together, cleaned up, went outside to play, came back in for lunch, played more, had dinner, helped clean up, took showers, watched t.v. for a bit before bedtime.

Every night Angie took us both to bed, and we picked which room we would be in when she read us our bedtime stories. We got kisses and hugs every night, and they told us they loved us every night. This was so foreign to both of us. We both became antsy and realized that this was all too good to be true.

After the first few weeks, something in me changed. My emotions were always fluctuating, like I was on a rollercoaster of emotions. I always wanted my sisters, and I would cry for them anytime I thought about them. I probably cried every single day for one reason or another. It's like I wanted them to know I was emotionally unstable right up front so they could decide to get rid of me sooner rather than later. I would tell them sometimes I hated them and I didn't want to live with them anymore. I never said stuff like that to any other family.

Maybe I had it built up inside me for so long, and I was finally out of danger. I knew they would never hurt me, so I let it all out. They didn't let me get away with my fits and anger, and anytime they tried to discipline me or have me sit in time out to calm down, I would threaten to call my social worker and have her come pick me up. I argued all the time. Anything they asked me to do or tried to tell me, I argued back just to cause a fight.

Every step I took was pushing me closer and closer to becoming the very thing I had been trying to avoid becoming. I was aware that if I kept going on my current path, I might ruin my chance of a new life. Years ago, I had made a decision to never become like my mother, so why was I now attempting to ruin everything positive I had achieved in my life? I wondered if there was anything I could to change who I would become one day. I was afraid that despite everything I had gone through, there might be a chance that I would end up like Beverly.

Maybe it was in my blood. I knew, though, that if I pushed this family away, I would be right back where I was and at that point, there would be no chance of being adopted. I would grow up in foster care and inevitably get thrown into the world with no support, and one day I would realize that I am the exact same person as Beverly.

Jack and Angie never gave up on us, though. They had rules and set boundaries. They had to un-teach years of bad habits and break us away from all the bad things so they could start to build us up into the people we were meant to be. For the first time in my life, I had people who wanted to fight for me, and I couldn't understand why they wanted to. I hated them for it. How could I sit there, feel sorry for myself, and drown myself in misery when I had two people who loved me unconditionally? The inability to do it drove me crazy and I couldn't take it anymore. I found comfort in retreating within my own head and exploring my own thoughts and ideas. It was something I was so used to doing.

I had separated myself from any reality, and they were forcing me back onto earth, onto solid ground. In hindsight, I can't understand why I couldn't just be happy, keep my mouth shut, and be grateful for what I was given.

I couldn't do it.

Even after I realized I was trying to sabotage everything, I argued every chance I got and had a smart-ass comment about everything. I couldn't help myself. If you push hard enough, people will always give up. They always did before. These people were no different. I knew they were no different. I have met enough people in my life to know they are all the same.

Growing up, I always had the same dream for as long as I could remember. I was five or six when I started having the dream.

In my dream, I was at a school, probably a made-up place. I was at the top of a big hill, not humongous but still relatively big, and it was a cloudy day. The ground was wet because it had just rained. I started out facing away from the playground on top of the hill. I looked out across this large expanse of grass beyond a fence.

When I turned around, I saw the Power Rangers fighting a monster. I knew I needed to get away from the fight, so I wouldn't get hurt or captured by the monster I felt was there for me. I ran down the hill towards a chain-link fence that stretched to the north and south. Beyond the chain-link fence, the sun was setting. I stopped running once I realized the hill was steep and muddy. I tried to walk down the hill as carefully as possible, and I leaned backward to help myself. It had just rained, though, and right where I was trying to walk was just mud. There was nothing for my feet to grip, and I slid on my side down the hill.

As I descended the hill, I picked up speed and slammed into the fence at the bottom. The fence rattled loudly as my body collided with it, and I looked back up the hill again, afraid I would see the monster coming after me. Once I realized the monster was still at the top and unaware of where I was, I looked around to see what was around me.

On either side of me were large bushes. My back was up against the fence and I was sitting in the mud. I could feel the cool, wet mud against my skin as I slid down.

As I attempted to wipe the mud off my body, I heard a rustling noise coming from the bushes, and I caught something moving out of the corner of my eye.

I looked to my left and saw something in the bushes.

It looked like someone I knew, and as the person crawled closer toward me, I realized it was Beverly.

She was crawling towards me, but she wasn't alive.

I could tell by her pale skin, the decay and rot all over her body, and her lifeless eyes. She had bruises and cuts all over her face. My eyes shifted down toward her hand, and I realized she was holding a large butcher's knife. I was frozen, unable to move. I could feel my heart thumping wildly in my chest.

Even if I could move, I wouldn't know what to do. She kept crawling toward me on her hands and knees. Her eyes were black and lifeless, and the way she smiled made me realize she was going to kill me. She started moving faster toward me and then lifted her arm up and tried to stab me with the knife. She missed, and I got up as quickly as I could and climbed the fence without looking back.

I scrambled over the fence and tried my hardest not to look back at where I had just been sitting. As I turned and started running, I felt like someone was close to me. I looked beside me and saw my little sister, Olivea, running along with me. She must have been with me the entire time following me. We didn't say a word to one another, but we both knew we were in this together and needed to get away.

I turned back one time and looked at the hill, hoping I would see where my Damien was. I saw the hill, and the fight was still happening, but no sign of my brother.

I took my sister's hand, and we both ran towards this city. Miles ahead, and all around us, was beautiful green grass, a vast field of it in all directions, except behind us. In front of us, the sky went from gray to yellow as the sky cleared up and the sun continued to set behind the city. Suddenly, I had a feeling that my foster mom, Donna, was behind us. When I turned back, I felt her presence, even though I couldn't actually see her. As I ran with my sister, the sound of my breath filled the air, becoming louder and faster with each step. Then, I woke up at the same spot every single time. I would lie in bed scared and tell myself over and over that it was just a bad dream.

Things like that always would bring me back to reality, almost like they grounded me like a weighted vest. That was my brain's way of making sure I never forgot. Even in my dreams, I could never escape my past. It is always there. You hear phrases like ghosts of the past or skeletons in your closet. The reference is always something scary because usually when you have ghosts in your past; they do just what ghosts do.

They haunt you, never leaving your side, clinging onto you, and using your body as their lifeblood.

That is what my ghosts did. At eight years old, I had too many ghosts to even know how to handle them. I let my feelings consume me sometimes, and it would get to where I would look for reasons to be sad. It's like I couldn't let myself go on and live a normal life. I had to keep torturing myself over and over to feel alive. I often didn't feel a lot, and at least when I forced myself to think about my past and feel sorry for myself, I could feel something.

My parents were the only thing that kept me from drowning. My mom or dad would dig me out of a closet or from under the bed, and I would have thought of some reason I was so upset, but it was all fake, and most days, it still is fake. All I wanted was for somebody to give me attention. All I wanted was for someone to ask me what happened, so I could finally feel the weight lifted off my chest. I didn't have it in me to feel sorry for myself. I wanted other people to feel sorry for me. Whenever I encountered someone, I would always find myself playing that game with them. It was a great feeling to finally have control and power over my own life.

The only thing that could ever really hurt was being alone. That was the one thing I have always been terrified of. I have never liked being alone, because then I end up back in my mind and back in the past.

CHAPTER 10

Over the following months, Damien and I lived with Jack and Angie to get a better feel about how we would all work together. Things began to change slowly. As we got to know each other, our trust in one another gradually grew. Although my brother and I still managed to get into trouble from time to time, my parents would always take the time to sit down with us and have a discussion about it. I sometimes wished they would have spanked us and sent us to bed early, but they always made us sit there and talk through it.

I loved our new home, and I never wanted to leave. I prayed all the time they would never give us back.

November 1997 came around, and it was a month before our final hearing for adoption. We had spent the summer and most of the fall together, and I think by then, my parents knew they weren't letting us go.

The news anchor who did our interview for "Home for Keeps" from WTOL 11 came back, and they did a video of my ninth birthday to air on the news. I was so excited when I found out that the news station would come to our house for my birthday party. I felt like a celebrity when they got to the house and set up the lights and cameras. It was exciting to see the news anchor again, and I could tell she was excited to see me and Damien. I opened presents first and the news anchor asked questions to my parents as they watched me open presents. It was the first birthday I remembered having and knowing that it would be on the news made it even more special.

Our parents talked about the first time we met, and how much they felt we belonged together. I opened a lot of presents and Damien watched for the most part, but then he jumped in and helped open the toys and put them together for me.

The news station aired my ninth birthday party in my new family's house later that week and I was so excited to watch it on the news. I was so embarrassed about one clip they had on the recording, but it was also hilarious after the fact.

I didn't remember asking Damien anything, but in the recording, as I was opening a present, I said, "Well, if you are such a great man, then come over here and give me a kiss."

Without hesitation, he said, "No."

I thought it was so funny that I said that and that he responded that way because it showed our relationship perfectly. We loved each other so much, but it didn't change the fact that I was the annoying little sister.

December finally came around, and it was time for our adoption. In the weeks leading up to our court date, Damien and I seemed to be getting ourselves into more and more trouble. I felt like we were constantly getting scolded for something, or having to sit in time-out regardless of what we did. Part of me wanted to leave Angie and Jack at times. I felt a strange mix of emotions leading up to the day of the court hearing; I knew that, for the first time in a long time, I had the power of choice. If I didn't want them to be my parents forever, I could say no, and that would be the end of it. The day before the final hearing, I thought about my birth parents, wondering where they were. As I thought about Beverly, I wondered if I would ever see her again. I was a little afraid that if someone adopted me, there would never be an opportunity for me to go back home, but I reminded myself that I didn't even know where she was and I would probably be better off without her.

We went to the Fulton County Courthouse for our final hearing. The judge first asked Angie and Jack if they wanted to adopt us and be our parents.

They both said yes without hesitation.

It was a good feeling to hear that and to know they really wanted me. The judge then asked me and Damien if we wanted Jack and Angela to be our new parents. We had a choice for the first time in a long time.

We both excitedly said, "Yes!"

It was nerve-wracking to think that I was going to be making it a permanent decision, and it was extremely frightening to me that these individuals who I had only known for a short amount of time were now going to be my mom and dad. The idea of them being my parents felt strange.

I felt it would be too awkward to call them mom and dad. It had been a long time since I had spoken the words 'mom' and 'dad' out loud, and I still could not bring myself to say it. They didn't mind that we still called them Angie and Jack even after the adoption, and I think that made me feel better knowing they didn't expect anything from us. They were willing to wait until I was ready, and that meant the world to me.

After we signed our papers, the judge let us sit in his chair and use the gavel. We both sunk into the huge chair, and I could hear the gentle creak of the leather as we shifted. We each took a turn hitting the gavel, listening to the satisfying sound it made as it echoed through the room. He gave each of us one to take home: one with a pink ribbon around it and one with a blue ribbon around it. I left the courthouse that day with a new name and a new life. That was the best day of my life.

After the adoption, things changed a little. I noticed that Jack and Angie felt more comfortable with us. We were more comfortable with them as well and that came with some issues because that was when we started pushing boundaries. They never let us get away with anything, though. They were very strict, and they did not take anything lightly. I realized that the longer we lived with them, the more we started to show ourselves and who we really were. They kept working regardless of how hard we made it for them. They kept tearing down walls we had put up and re-shaping us into new people. We had chores we had to do every day and a routine every day when we came home. Angela pushed routines.

Our dad was the same.

Jack was hard on us, but he had high expectations for us. Even though it would have been much simpler for him to allow us to get by for the next nine to ten years until adulthood, he had a good sense of what we could accomplish, and he knew we had the potential to do better. He made sure that we both understood it as well.

It was funny to think back on those years after I became an adult. I don't know if Jack knew what to do with us, so he did what he felt needed to be done. He wasn't always hard, so don't think that for a second. My dad had an amazing ability to be both fun and playful, especially during our time spent together. He liked to spend time with my brother and me. I have a lot of memories of us wrestling around and being loud and my mom yelling at my dad and us to quit wrestling and roughhousing because we would get so loud.

A lot of times we would start out wrestling, and it would turn into a full-blown tickle war. My Dad was so ticklish, especially on his feet that he would flail around if my brother and I tickled them. Even though I despised being tickled, I still had a good time when my dad and I would play together and we got into tickle fights.

Every Sunday, my dad and I would spend hours poring over the newspapers for coupons, then head out to the grocery store together. I enjoyed sitting next to him, flipping through the paper, and cutting out the coupons that we would use.

At the store, we went from sample stand to sample stand, and my dad would always crack jokes while conversing with the people working at the store, as well as the other shoppers roaming around.

I could not contain my laughter as he joked around, making it sound like we were just there to enjoy a simple lunch. He would joke to people and tell them about how Damien and I kept following him around all the time, but he didn't know us. Our dad had a sixth sense for finding stores with the most delicious samples. His enthusiasm could turn the day into an amusing adventure.

When we went shopping, we always made sure to explore everything each aisle had to offer, and he had a very exciting and fun personality. Understanding the difficult times we'd been through, he made sure to make us feel appreciated and accepted by going out of his way to show us love.

Whatever I went through as a child wasn't wiped away after I was adopted. Still, living with a family who loved me exponentially more than my birth parents ever could have, I knew all the trials we went through were worth it. If I could go back and go through all the pain again, knowing I would get the parents I have now, I would do it all over again. They were worth every day of waiting and gave me a childhood-at least the end of my childhood- that many kids would dream of.

We would snuggle up with Angela every night, and the feeling of being next to her while she read was comforting. Our regular trips to the library would always include us picking up the Goosebumps and choose-your-own-adventure books. My brother and I would go and get comfortable in either his bed or mine, and our mother would let us take turns deciding what path to take in the Goosebumps books. Every night she would make sure we were tucked in and secure, giving us both hugs and kisses and reminding us of how much she loved us.

I spent most of my childhood hiding in dark corners, behind doors, and under beds. I always listened, feeling the floor below me for something different; movement, vibrations, the sound of footsteps coming towards me. I always lived in fear of being seen because being seen instantly raised my chances of getting in trouble or being hurt. So, it was better to be unseen.

At the age of nine, I was entering into a new stage of life. I no longer had to spend any more days worrying if I would remain in foster care for the rest of my life. I didn't ask for a mom or dad anymore when I said my prayers at night. My entire world had changed, and it was such an amazing feeling.

There were still bad days. Although I still felt the pain of losing my birth parents and siblings, I could feel myself getting better day by day.

A year after I had been adopted into the family, our mom and dad sat me and Damien down in the living room and told us we were going to have a baby sibling. I could not believe it. I was so excited at the thought of having a baby in the house and having another sibling that I would grow up with. At the time, I didn't know my mom's struggles with having a baby prior to us being adopted. Nine months later, we welcomed my little brother, Michael, into the world.

On Thanksgiving Day in 1998, my brother was born, and I could feel my heart swell with love. He was perfect in every way. I loved playing with him and spending time with him. My mom was very clear with the boundaries she set for my brother and me, reassuring us that he was our sibling and not another child for us to take care of. It was a relief not having to constantly worry about taking care of a baby. I could enjoy playing with him and teaching him new things, without the pressure of the everyday responsibilities of caring for a baby.

Over the years, I had the privilege of watching him grow up, and my love for him only deepened in the first couple of years. With the passing of time, it became increasingly more difficult to show him love on certain days. On some occasions, I found myself feeling a jealous of him. Michael was the center of attention and during those times, I felt like he was what they wanted most. I was terrified that they would understand that they had taken on too much responsibility and, with the birth of their own baby, they would consider giving us back. As Michael began to grow older and transition into his toddler years, I started taking my frustration out on him in the form of bullying and meanness, leading him to tears.

I could never understand why I was suddenly being so mean to him. Sometimes I hated myself for picking on him and making him cry because I knew he didn't do anything to deserve it. Sometimes he would walk up to me to give me a hug or want me to pick him up, and I would push him away.

He would start crying and I wouldn't always feel bad even after he started crying. I started to wonder if this is what my birth mother was like and as I got older and thought back on the times I bullied him; I wondered if that trait was something deeply rooted in me.

I wondered if Beverly was ever mean to me and my siblings in that same way and thought that maybe I was acting this way because it was who I was. I loved kids, so I didn't understand what made me want to be mean to my little brother. He was such a kind-hearted and well-mannered child, which made me feel even worse for treating him poorly despite his innocence.

Even though I tried to be good, I still managed to get into trouble at times, and each time I did, it caused me to resent Michael even more. Over the years, I convinced myself that if I was Angie and Jack's real child, then they would never get mad at me, and they would never discipline me or yell at me. I couldn't stop myself from thinking it, even though I knew it wasn't true.

CHAPTER 11

Have you ever revisited old memories and felt as though they were distant, almost like a dream?

That was how my life felt in the years leading up to being a teenager. It was difficult for me to accept that anything I went through was real.

As a teenager, my emotions would change, like the phases of the moon. During one week, I felt as if I could almost forget the traumatic experiences I had as a child, allowing me to be genuinely happy and carefree. Gradually, in the week that followed, my mind would accept that all of it was real, just like the waxing and waning of the moon, and I would come to terms with the fact that it was not a dream.

This was my life for years; the same patterns on repeat. It became predictable, but there was nothing I could do to stop it. When the reality of my life hit me again, and the next phase came, I knew it would be bad for a while. I had to ride out the wave, regardless of what was going on in my life.

It always passed though, and somehow I would be happy again, despite knowing it was all real. The memories and the experiences would distance themselves enough so they weren't so present at the forefront of my thoughts. They would kind of hang back and linger in the corners of my mind. The pain and the sadness were still there. For a brief moment, I could keep the reality of my past at a distance, allowing myself to feel as if nothing had ever happened. The next cycle always came, though, no matter what.

When I was thirteen, I finally had friends I could talk to about things. It turned out that none of my friends had experienced the things that I went through. I had been living in this fantasy world where nothing affected me because I assumed everyone went through similar things.

My normal had been so blown out of proportion that hearing other girls' normal shook me. I found myself overwhelmed with feelings of jealousy. It was a difficult thing to accept that everybody else around me had experienced a normal upbringing and I had not, and what was even more difficult to comprehend was that I had never even realized what had happened to me. I didn't think much of the abuse I experienced because I considered it to be a normal part of life.

In eighth grade, became friends with a girl from school, and soon enough we had become best friends, being closer than ever. Shelly and I always found something fun to do and somewhere along the way, we became like sisters. Shelly was my ride or die friend. We got into a lot of trouble together, but I wouldn't have taken any of it back because some of my best memories as a teenager were with her. I was drawn to her because she was fearless and she wasn't afraid to do anything. She still is that way today. It was one thing I admired about her, and why I wanted to be her friend.

She didn't care what anyone thought of her, and as far as I know, never has. She and I would go to the Coffee House at night at my church. It was open once a week for the youth to come and spend time. We'd always sneak off and go for a walk, head over to the railroad tracks, and have a cigarette.

It seemed to always work that way, though. I wasn't part of the typical cliques like the athletes, the pretty and popular kids, or the nerds. Growing up before I was adopted, I didn't have anyone encouraging me or teaching me sports, and this is probably why I wasn't very good at them. As a kid, I was teased a lot for my crazy frizzy hair that I couldn't control, or the clothes that I wore, or that I talked all the time and would often annoy people.

One of the first times I went to the Coffee House at my church I began to think about Cain. I walked to the bathroom, and two of my friends that were there that night followed me. As I entered the bathroom, a wave of sadness washing over me. I sat down in the corner, feeling the carpet beneath me, and put my head to my knees, the sound of my sobs filling the room. That day, I felt a sudden realization of everything I had gone through, and it overwhelmed me. I realized Cain had a more significant hold on me than I ever thought he did. I was often able to make his actions seem reasonable. *He didn't beat me or hit me. Sometimes, he was really nice to me.*

My two friends stayed with me and offered comfort while I was crying in the bathroom. Another person came in to the restroom telling me my mom and dad were looking for me. One girl hurried out and got my mom. When she walked into the bathroom, she looked less than impressed with my dramatic debut. I told her I needed to talk to her, so we both walked out to the car in the parking lot, passing my dad on our way out the door. She told him we needed to talk in private and asked him to wait inside.

When we got to the car, she asked, "What's going on with you?"

"I want to tell you something about what happened when I lived with one of my foster families."

"Okay, what is it?" she replied.

"When I lived with the Clarks, my foster brother Cain molested me," I said with tears still in my eyes.

I wanted to tell her more, but I was too afraid to tell her any details or to even tell her the truth about how bad it was. I didn't mention how many times, and I didn't say anything about what he would do to me.

My mom didn't look surprised, but I knew she didn't know because I had never talked to her about it before. Later in life, it dawned on me that she had likely come to the assumption based on her work in social work and familiarity with the foster care system. I can still picture the look on my mom's face as she said what came next.

"You can continue to feel sorry for yourself and cry and play the victim over something that happened years ago, or you can realize that shit happens. Bad things happen to people every single day, and you need to learn to move on and cope with what happened so you can live a normal life."

Her response completely devastated me, but I also knew that she was not wrong.

My mom was never very good at expressing sympathy for any of us kids, and she was sternly against coddling us.

I didn't understand her response that night.

All I wanted was for her to feel sorry for me and let me tell her about everything. It might have helped just being able to talk about it, but then what? Any way I looked at it, she was right. I could not let myself live as a victim and continue to feel sorry for myself and live in a constant state of 'woe is me'.

I listened to what she had to say and took it seriously. Still, I would cry about it things sometimes, and there were days I would feel sorry for myself. I was a teenager, so what else would you expect?

Drugs were one factor that made an impact on my life during that year. Later on in the school year, I tried smoking pot for the first time and, besides that, we started using cocaine on a regular basis. What Damien and I were doing wouldn't have normally been seen as a detrimental problem, since we were both at the age when kids typically start experimenting. I am not sure if my parents were really strict or if it had more to do with their fear of us having issues with addiction. I don't think either of us new back then, that addiction is often hereditary.

After school, Damien and I would come home and do a couple of lines of coke and do stupid stuff together. One day after school we had snorted coke and then hung out in my bedroom trying to think of stuff to do because we were bored. Damien always kept everything in my room because he had been in a lot of trouble over the last few years, and our mom and dad searched his room regularly. We tried to make fireballs with my mousse bottle and a lighter.

After Damien did it twice, I took the stuff from him, and he started teasing me jokingly. I turned the bottle, pointing it at his face, and lit the fumes. I was messing around and didn't actually want to get the fire close to his face, but I accidentally burned Damien's eyebrows and a little of the front of his hair.

The entire upstairs reeked like burned hair, and I started panicking and apologizing to Damien. We both tried to think of how we were going to hide the smell from our parents. We couldn't hide it, though. They found out what we were doing, and we were both in trouble.

It only took a few months before my school found out what I was doing, and then, in turn, the school told my parents. I was mortified when the principal told me everything he knew and how he found out. He only knew about the weed at that time, but I still begged him not to tell my parents.

My dad worked at the school, and that made it that much worse because he knew the principal personally. I begged Mr. Collin's to not say anything to my dad, but he said he had no choice.

Later that night, as Damien and I sat in the dining room with our parents, pastor, and a police officer, I realized what was happening to me. I had tears streaming down my face, looking at the bowl on the table in front of me that my dad found in Damien's room.

Looking up, I saw tears in my dad's eyes, and I looked at my mom next to him, crying. I told them we had been using coke, and the look in my parents' eyes broke me. *How could I do this to them?*

I realized I had turned out to be my mother. I was using drugs to numb my pain. I had been lying and stealing too. After living with my mom and dad for almost five years, I realized that maybe it didn't matter that I had been away from my birth mom for almost ten years and out of the system for five years.

Despite my mom and dad's guidance for nearly five years, I still found myself on a path of self-destruction. That day, I realized that if I was not intentional about not turning into my birth mother, it would be very easy to end up on that path. It scared me to think such small choices could impact my life so drastically.

Somehow, I was making some of the same mistakes that she had made in her life, and I didn't even realize what I was doing. I told my parents about everything else because I wanted to start over, and I wanted them to know everything. I realized I needed help, and they wouldn't be able to help me if I didn't tell them everything.

That night, my brother and I realized that what we did was terrible and you could see the guilt on both of our faces. Had we not seen our mom and dad react in that way, I don't think we would have given much thought to how we had been acting. We had never seen our mom and dad that upset, and we had never done anything bad enough that our parents called the police and our pastor. Having our pastor there was more humiliating than having the police there and I felt so ashamed that my parents felt they had to resort to calling our pastor as well.

That night, as I put my room back together that my dad had torn apart earlier, I prayed. I begged and pleaded with God to make a change in me. I desperately hoped that I would not end up like Beverly and be in the same situation. However, I was terrified that it might already be too late.

CHAPTER 12

In my senior year of high school, I had to start thinking about what I was going to do after graduating. When my parents had asked me what I wanted to do with my life, I had told them I wanted to be an author. My mom told me that I needed to grow up and be realistic, so I knew I had to start thinking of other career options. After a couple of months, I thought seriously about joining the military.

I was at school one day and saw a recruiter in the lunchroom.

I walked up to him and realized the banner read 'Marines' and said, "Oh, never mind, I thought you were the Army."

The recruiter chuckled and said, "What's so great about the Army? You don't want to talk to the Marines?"

Joining the Marine Corps had never entered my thoughts until then. I was familiar with the Army and I thought that this was the path I was set on taking. Following my brief conversation with the recruiter that day, I took some time to think about my options.

Weeks later, my dad went with me to meet the recruiter. After we returned home, my dad said, "I think maybe you should consider the Air Force or the Navy."

"I really think I want to join the Marine Corps, though. Everything the recruiter talked about is everything I need."

"I am worried that the Marine Corps is going to be too hard for you. The Air Force or Navy would be a better fit."

I had my mind made up, though. I could tell my mom was sick at the thought of me joining the Marine Corps. They both told me they didn't think I could do it because of how hard the boot camp would be, and that made me want to do it even more.

By my senior year of high school, a lot had changed for me. The year before, my parents adopted my little brother, Jax.

Jax was the most adorable baby I had ever seen in my life. He had bright red hair and the biggest blue eyes I had ever seen. When my mom told me about the neglect and abuse Jax had gone through with his birth mother, I was heartbroken. When I saw the one-year-old boy, I couldn't comprehend how any person could disregard him and leave him alone in a parking lot like his own mother did. From the day Jax became part of our family after being adopted, I felt an immediate and overwhelming love for him.

The next summer, before my senior year, my mom gave birth to my other little brother, John.

John was a surprise baby, but he was a very welcome surprise. I was so excited when John was born and I absolutely loved being a big sister to all three of my little brothers. Michael was about seven years old and I loved him so much. He was such a good kid, and he loved hanging out with me. I had friends that would come to my house and hang out during high school and Michael was always my sidekick. My friends loved hanging out with him, and I loved having him around.

Since I was older when Jax and John came, I started babysitting more and doing more with my brothers to help my mom and dad out. I loved helping with my brothers, and because there was such a huge age gap between me and the two younger boys, I thought of them as my kids. I knew they weren't mine, and I never had to act in a way that would make me seem like their mother at any point. As the older sibling, it gave me the opportunity to have fun and be able to do the exciting things with them.

Having my little brothers changed my mind about wanting to have a family of my own. By the time I had completed high school, I became sure that I did not want to have any children of my own. I had decided to be the best big sister I could be and take care of my little brothers for as long as I could.

Joining the military didn't scare me at the time. I did not have any goals to get married or have children at that time, and I believed that if I worked hard, then I could potentially have a long and successful career in the military.

When the recruiter came to our house to meet my parents a week later, I was more convinced that this was what I needed to do with my life. I was nervous, but I felt that this was my only option. My parents had told me that after graduation I had to move out unless I was going to college full time or was working full time. The only jobs I had experience in were restaurant work, babysitting, and cleaning houses, so I knew finding a job that would pay enough would not happen. I was also terrified of going to college. At the time, I knew I wasn't smart enough.

My grades in high school were not great, and I never applied myself. I knew myself well enough to know that there was no way I would take college seriously and be accountable for myself. I felt that if I had gone to college, I would get into the party scene and end up failing. On top of that, I didn't know what I wanted to do for the rest of my life. I had thoughts about different degrees I could get, but I felt that I was not disciplined enough to follow through. I spent most of my years as a child fantasizing about being married, becoming a housewife, and being a mother. Once I got into my senior year, reality set in, and I realized that what I imagined for my life in the years before was not realistic.

Joining the military made sense, and I figured if I ended up hating it and not wanting to make a career of it, then it would at least give me time to figure my life out. I didn't have a lot figured out when I was eighteen, but I knew I had to do something great with my life. I wanted to keep my promise that I had made to myself as a little girl.

My junior and senior years were by far the best years of high school. I was finally getting out of the goofy middle school phase and becoming a woman. School was never easy for me, and in general, my grades were pretty bad. I loved school because that was time away from home, and I could be around my friends. My junior year, my favorite class was health, an elective I chose to take with our science teacher, who didn't require much effort to pass the class.

The first time I saw Joe, I remember his infectious smile that made me feel warm inside. He was sitting in the front row of desks, and I settled into my seat a few rows back.

I couldn't take my eyes off him when we were in the same room. He was a freshman, but his tousled brown hair and contagious laugh made him the cutest boy in the school. His kindness towards everyone, including me, was magnetic, drawing me closer to him. His eyes were big and dark brown and they were accentuated by his long, curled eyelashes. Joe's deep brown eyes were the first thing that caught my attention. His eyes held a warm and inviting kindness within them. When he was happy and laughing, you could see the light in his eyes and hear his laughter filling the room. Whenever we had a conversation, his eyes had a certain look, almost like he was playfully teasing me when he looked at me.

His smile was so infectious that I couldn't help but love it. He had big lips and there was a pouty shape to his mouth, but that would disappear when he laughed or smiled. Whenever our paths crossed, he had a genuine smile on his face that made me want to be around him more. His energy was contagious. It was no surprise that everyone loved him.

His personality was so attractive that it made everyone want to be his friend, and he was very accepting of everyone who wanted to be his friend. He didn't care about what anyone thought; he was his own person living his life.

He wore skater shirts and shoes, completing his look with a pair of baggy jeans that hung from his hips. Joe's style was always so casual, like he had just rolled out of bed and thrown on the first thing he saw.

I would always have one of my best friends, Mona, bring me clothes to school, and I would change in the bathroom before Mr. Johnson's class. I wanted Joe to notice me, so I would wear tight, low-cut shirts with lace accents. My parents never gave me the option to dress as I wanted to and that style was off-limits to me. My dad chose all of my clothes, which is why my wardrobe was so modest. During our free periods in school, Joe and I would talk occasionally, but we were never part of the same social group. I was friends with a lot of his friends, yet for some reason we never ended up spending any time together outside of the classes we had together.

I would sit in class, my eyes tracing over his face, arms, and hair as I tried to memorize every detail. Even though I already was in high school, most of the guys didn't take any notice of me and certainly did not express any interest in me. Joe at least acknowledged my existence and would talk to me sometimes. I had always hoped that one day Joe would ask me out, but he never did.

We stayed friends and would talk in the hallways or in class if we saw each other, but that was it. He was the only guy in high school I had ever had an interest in, but I didn't think he was ever interested in me. I pushed him out of my head and started focusing more on my own life.

Back then, it had never crossed my mind that one day we would be together. Of course, it was something I wished would happen, but I didn't think there would be any way our paths would cross again one day. I didn't think that one day we would be together and have a house and a life together.

By the time I graduated high school, Joe was just some guy that I knew. We were in school together, but our paths never intertwined back then.

Before my graduation, my older sister, Jamie, asked me if I wanted to meet Beverly. We went out one day to spend time with each other since it had been a couple of years since we had seen each other.

At first, I was confused because I didn't know Jamie knew where she was. She had recently started seeing Beverly more, and I couldn't believe it. I was terrified that my parents would find out, but I didn't think I would ever get another chance like this.

"Yea, we can go see her. I would like to meet her."

"Okay, it isn't far from where we are now. She will be so excited to see you Sheila!"

"Will it be weird if we just show up there? I don't want to make things awkward."

"No, not at all. It will be cool. She will be excited, I promise," Jamie responded.

I felt sick to my stomach. Images of Beverly flashed in my mind. First came a memory from when I lived there, and then came the memory of the last time I had seen her on the sidewalk outside of Children Services. I wondered if she looked much different. It had been about twelve years since the last time I saw her face. *I wonder what she looks like now. I wonder what she will think of me when she sees me.* At that moment, I was very thankful that I had taken the time to dress nicely and that my hair had cooperated that day.

We pulled up to the house and parked on the road. Jamie got out and led the way. Kids were playing outside, and I was not sure who they were at first, but Jamie introduced me to them, and I realized the girl was my little sister, Emily. As I saw Emily standing in front of me, my mind went blank for a moment. I couldn't believe that the baby girl I had lost so long ago was now a teenager. My heart was racing, and my palms were sweaty. I felt a lump in my throat and tears prickling at the corners of my eyes.

The baby girl who had been taken from me so long ago was standing in front of me now as a teenager. I couldn't believe how much she had changed and grown. On our drive there, it didn't occur to me I would see Emily when we got there. Until that point, I wasn't positive that Emily still lived with Beverly. I had seen my sister Jamie occasionally over the years, but she had never mentioned anything about Emily or Beverly.

It was overwhelming seeing Emily for the first time after so many years, and I could feel my heartbeat increasing as I tried to process that I was actually looking at my little sister. I felt a tightness in my chest as I took a deep breath and tried to mentally prepare for meeting Beverly. There were two little boys there as well, running around outside and playing. Jamie introduced me to Jeff and Rylie as my little brothers, although I had never met them before.

I was shocked because I didn't realize Beverly had more kids after Emily was born. I had no idea that I had two younger brothers until I was standing in front of them. It was a surreal moment, and I really did not know how to react, so I just

introduced myself to them. As I was trying to process everything, Jamie had me follow her to the front door and into the
house. I felt like I was moving in slow motion, almost as if I
was in a dream.

Jamie took me to the living room, and Beverly was there,
seated on the sofa, watching television. As soon as I saw her, I
knew who she was, but she didn't look the same as I remembered. The first thing I noticed was her hair, which was much
shorter than I had seen in pictures and a different color than
what I had remembered.

I had a mental image of a more glowing and youthful version of the woman that I was seeing. I was not expecting to
see this woman looking as she did now, with her graying hair
and a more aged and worn look to her. She still looked good
considering her age and what kind of life she had led, but I
felt like she was not my mom, but rather some version of her
that wasn't quite right.

In the moments before she even embraced me, I realized
that this woman was a stranger, and any fantasy in my head
leading up to that moment of seeing my mom again and feeling her hold me in her arms again after all these years faded.
When Jaime told her who I was, she shot up from her seat,
her eyes wide with shock.

She kept saying, "Oh my God," as she wrapped her arms
around me and hugged me.

Her voice was unfamiliar, with a rough timbre that was un-
like anything I had expected. She spoke with a gravelly voice,
and I could have sworn her voice used to be more high-pitched
and melodic.

The sensation of her embrace was not what I had expected, but I still returned her hug. I felt like I was in a vacuum that was sucking all the air out of my lungs. The air around me felt heavy as I took shallow, labored breaths. Beverly's sobs sounded like a broken record, repeating the same words over and over, but they couldn't reach me.

The hug felt stiff and uncomfortable, and I could feel my body tensing up, eager to get away. When I looked at her, I thought I should know her, but there was nothing familiar about her. As she held me in her arms and her forced, hollow sobs echoed in my ears, I couldn't help but feel numb.

Even though I felt uncomfortable, I stayed and talked with Beverly. I listened to Beverly as she talked about how much she missed me and how happy she was to see me again.

She showed me pictures of me hanging on her refrigerator, some of which were recent pictures. I could guess that my sisters had given her photos of me I had mailed to them over the years.

We didn't stay long since my parents were expecting me to be home soon. We said our goodbyes, and Jamie drove me back home. Being back in the car and back on the road gave me a huge sense of comfort and I felt much better. I felt like I had been holding my breath since we walked in that house, and I finally could let my breath out and get oxygen into my lungs. I felt like I had been suffocating being inside that house, and I knew I never wanted to go back there again.

Months later, on the ride up to Detroit with my recruiter, my stomach was in knots. I couldn't believe I was doing this. *Once you sign the papers, you can't just change your mind.* I knew I was in this, and there was no backing out. At the Marine Depot Station, standing before an Officer of the Marine Corps, I took my oath.

The following day, we headed to the airport. We got on the plane to head to Parris Island Marine Corps Recruit Training in South Carolina. A boy I met the night before sat beside me on the airplane and told me what to expect so I would not be so nervous. He had flown a bunch of times before. That was my first time being on an airplane, and I was nervous.

As the airplane began to move, I could feel the rumbling as the airplane taxied to the runway. Even though I was hesitant about it at first, I ended up loving it. I felt the force of the airplane push me back into my seat slightly as the plane took off, and suddenly I could tell that we were off of the ground. I felt a weird flip in my stomach as the plane ascended and I could see out the window that we were in the air. All of my nerves left, and I decided that I absolutely loved being on a plane.

Once we landed in South Carolina, we all boarded a bus late at night and headed to Parris Island. The bus ride was about two hours from the airport. It was freezing on the bus, and, of course, I was wearing a light T-Shirt since it was the middle of July. I spent the entire bus ride shivering and huddled into myself because I was so cold. I was so tired I tried to sleep as much as possible, but the cold made it hard for me to sleep.

I would drift off for a few minutes and the cold would wake me up again. As we got close to Parris Island, I couldn't shake the feeling of dread that settled heavy in my chest, and eventually, the tears came. I thought about my little brothers, and I realized I already missed them. My heart was racing as I felt my nervousness increasing, and a sudden wave of fear overcame me. I didn't know what I had just gotten myself into.

We got onto base and pulled up to a large building. As we waited for the bus doors to open, I couldn't help but notice the tension in the air. A male Drill Instructor stormed onto the bus, his presence commanding attention. He screamed as loud as he could in his froggy voice for everyone to get on their feet and grab their belongings. He barked orders to file off the bus. I scrambled to gather my things and make my way down the aisle, but the DI was already in my face, counting down the seconds in this bull-frog voice until I was off the bus.

Once we were all outside, the DI barked at us to stand on a set of yellow footprints in front of the administration building. Everything in my life changed in just an instant. We all walked inside and went through hours and hours of paperwork, processing, screaming, more paperwork. Drill instructors were everywhere. They tried to break you the moment you stepped on those footprints.

The first few days were like a nightmare.

I was in an open barracks with 70-plus other women and girls much like myself. Some you could look at and know they would never make it. I wondered if I was one of those girls.

I thought about my family often, my baby brothers, my parents, and my older brother. I missed them with every fiber of my being. It was as if a part of me was missing. I couldn't help but wonder if I had made a mistake by coming here. The first week was hard because everything was new and nothing made sense. There was constant screaming and chaos. The second week was harder because I was homesick. I wanted to hold my brothers again so badly. I wanted to be in my house again and be with my family.

I knew boot camp would not be easy, but I didn't expect to miss my family so much. I didn't expect those three months to drag on for so long. It felt like I was on that island for six months, and almost every day was hell. Each week felt like an eternity, and by the third week, I felt like I had made the biggest mistake of my life.

Every night, I cried in my bunk and wrote letters home under my blanket using a flashlight. I wanted my family so much, and writing was the only thing I could do to help ease the pain.

After what felt like an eternity, it was finally the last week of boot camp. I looked different, felt different, and acted different. The person I was before I arrived on the island was gone, and in its place was a new, improved version of me. Bootcamp had broken me down and rebuilt me into a new person. I was still me in a lot of ways, but there was a shift in my mindset. Everything felt different, and the way I thought had completely transformed.

During the last week, we had to go through the Crucible before we could participate in the graduation ceremony. It was the most grueling two days of my life, but I got through it. The Crucible was over, and I had my Eagle, Globe, and Anchor handed to me by one of my drill instructors during the ceremony.

As the emblem was placed in my hand, I suddenly saw Beverly's and Victor's faces cross through my mind. My mind switched, and then I saw Cain and his parents. Then, I saw the Kessler's. It hurt to think about any of the families I had lived with growing up, but for some reason, some hurt more than others. I wished I hadn't thought of them that day, but I did.

I imagined they were there watching me as I went from being a recruit to a Marine. I envisioned them looking at me with admiration, filled with remorse for their behavior towards me when I was a child. As I thought about how they would react if they were to ever find out that what they put me through didn't break me, I decided the next chapter of my life was going to be personal. I was going to get my revenge in the only way I knew how.

Even though I was tired, hungry, and in pain, it was the most rewarding day of my life. After what felt like an eternity, I finally made it to the end. I accomplished what I had set out to do.

As I stood in that spot, a feeling of pride rushed through me when I was called a Marine for the first time.

It was by far the proudest day of my entire life. I never felt the swell of pride as I did that day, and I let the tears flow down my face in pure happiness that I made it.

Not a single moment of it was easy, but I made it.

Later that day, I got to be reunited with my family. I wrapped my little brothers in my arms and held on to each of them, soaking in that moment for as long as I could.

I hugged my parents and held on, trying to stay in that moment for as long as I could. They were my family now, and they were the only family that mattered to me. None of the families I lived with before them mattered anymore. They were there, and that was all that mattered to me. They didn't have to make the sixteen hour drive to be there for my graduation, but they did. And I realized that they really would do anything for me.

They told me how proud they were of me, and that made me even more proud of myself. The next day, we had our graduation ceremony and after that; I was able to go home with my parents. They gave my platoon ten days of leave before heading to our MOS schools.

A BRIEF SILENCE

CHAPTER 13

The first time I met Matt, it was such a chance encounter. I was stationed in Okinawa, Japan while I was serving in the military. It was my first duty station, and I was very nervous about being in the field for the first time and also being in another country. It was exciting and new, but it made me feel very anxious at the same time. Once I got to Okinawa, I was separated from almost everyone from my Military Occupational Specialist school. Many of the Marines I was in school with went to Okinawa as well, but they were in another unit.

I was taken aback by Okinawa's breathtaking beauty from the moment I arrived. Okinawa had a distinct and unique smell, a mixture of salty ocean air, fresh vegetation, and the scent of traditional Okinawan foods like pork and seaweed. Okinawa was known for its delicious and healthy cuisine, including dishes like Okinawan soba, sushi, goya champuru, and taco rice. One of my favorite restaurants that I discovered quickly was Ichi Ban CoCos. It was an amazing curry house that was known for its chicken cutlet curry dishes. They often made these dishes with fresh local ingredients and reflect the island's cultural heritage.

The island's air was thick from the humidity and I could feel the sticky air on my skin, even in the early months of the year. In Ohio, the snow and frigid temperatures were still present. Whenever I ventured off base to explore the island more in my first few months, the heat was relieved by the ocean breeze, which carried with it the sound of waves crashing in the distance. I stepped onto the sand of the island's beach, feeling the warmth on my feet, and the coolness of the water lapping against my toes for the first time, and I knew I would never want to leave that place. The island is also home to many beautiful gardens and parks.

Lush, green hills rose from the coast, covered in dense vegetation and dotted with colorful flowers. Traditional red-tiled roofs could be seen on many of the buildings and houses in the cramped neighborhoods away from the city, while neon lights and billboards light up the bustling city streets at night when I went into the city. Exploring away from the military bases, I got to see firsthand the beautiful Japanese villages with their ancient culture.

One of the popular places for military personnel to party or go out drinking was called Gate Street. The street was lined with bars on the back side of one of the Air Force bases. The Japanese-style bars in the area had a distinctive smell of sake and cigarettes, popular among military personnel and locals.

I was working for the Air Traffic Control unit in the Aviation Supply Squadron. During that time, I lived in a different barracks from most of the people I went to MOS school with.

When I arrived at my new unit, it surprised me to find that only one person from my MOS school was in the same barracks and unit as me. I discovered that there had been a mix-up with my duty orders, so I had been assigned to the wrong unit for almost four months while I was waiting for the mistake to be corrected.

I had been in the ATC unit for a couple of months already, and one day my Corporal ordered parts from the main Supply Squadron. Later that day, two Marines showed up in a delivery van. The two Marines got out and opened up the back doors and hopped inside to unload. I walked up with a couple of Marines I worked with to help unload the van. Handing boxes out from the back of the van, the Marine turned around and gave one to his colleague. I looked at him and I couldn't shake the eerie feeling of Déjà vu that suddenly came over me.

Everything felt like it was in a standstill, and I had this strong intuition that I had already encountered him and we were both meant to be there that day. When I saw him, I was shocked by the familiarity of his face, as if I had known him all my life. I never forgot his face and that moment. Looking back on that moment years later, I would remember that moment, and it made me think that somehow that day I was seeing my future.

The moment I entered the building for MALS-26, I was welcomed by the same Marine I had seen in the delivery van a couple of months prior. I instantly remembered how we knew each other, and the same inexplicable feeling I had experienced when I saw him for the first time came flooding back. Again, I had a very encouraging feeling that I was exactly where I was supposed to be at that moment.

He introduced himself as PFC Martinez and offered his hand to me.

Matt had a lean, athletic frame, and his dark eyes filled with curiosity as he looked at me. His russet brown eyes drew me in as he talked. He had thin lips and perfect teeth. His jaw was prominent and gave him a strong, masculine appearance.

"I'm PFC Wolpert," I responded as I shook his hand.

He spoke, his voice deep and inviting, while he gestured with his head for me to follow him. Now and then, he would flash a sly smile, and I could tell that he was completely confident of himself. He pretended to be timid at times, but I could tell it was an act. He stood a couple inches above me and he had dark golden skin. It was summer and his sleeves on his dessert cami blouse were rolled up. I could make out the contours of his thin but muscular arms and the veins that snaked from his forearm to his hands.

PFC Martinez showed me around and took me to each department. He was very talkative, which was fine with me, and his enthusiastic demeanor made it easy to talk with him. He seemed like a young, fun, outgoing kid who was upbeat about everything. I could tell he felt comfortable around me because he had no issues invading my personal space. He maintained strong eye contact with me when he talked. It made me uncomfortable because I was not used to direct eye contact, but it made me even more uncomfortable because he was very handsome, and I did not want to look at him any longer than I had to. Once he noticed I was getting uncomfortable, he would give this innocent half-smile before he looked away.

In my new department, I found myself surrounded by Marines I had gone to school with. But out of all of them, my best friend was PFC Thornton, or Shia, as he preferred to be called. Despite his closed posture and unsociable demeanor, I gravitated towards him and he took me under his wing, showing me the ropes of the department.

It took a while for him to open up, but once he did, we became inseparable. I admired his intelligence and how effortlessly he seemed to understand things. My mom even suggested that I should date him, but I never saw him as more than a friend. Shia became my best friend. I liked him so much because he was everything I wished I could have been.

Along with Thornton, PFC Marshall and PFC Martinez were part of our group. We spent most of our downtime after work together. Martinez's first name was Mateo, but he went by Matt. Marshall was initially closer to Shia and me, but since he was best friends with Martinez, he became part of our group, too.

Despite my close friendship with Martinez, he began asking me out on dates, and each time he did, I felt uneasy. No matter how persistent he was, I always said no.

It didn't take long for me to realize how other people viewed him. It changed my opinion of him and made me not interested in ever dating him. He was not the type of person who could be friends with anyone, and a lot of the people I worked with didn't like him at all.

Gradually, our friendship seemed to shift as Matt's behavior began to change. After months of being friends with him, I realized he was no longer the happy, upbeat person I had first met. I went with Martinez and a few of our friends sightseeing around Okinawa, and we went to some amazing places.

One of our stops was at a Japanese castle, and it was such a beautiful place. It had Asian culture in every piece of it, and I was in awe. Martinez kept his headphones on the entire time we walked through the castle, and I felt like he was doing it for attention. He had a pouty, dejected look on his face, and every time I looked at him, I got annoyed with his moodiness.

He didn't smile much anymore, and when he hung out with our group of friends, he had his headphones on most of the time and didn't engage with us much.

Part of me wondered if he acted that way because he kept asking me out and I kept saying no, but the way he was acting irritated me more and made me not want to be around him at all.

Weeks after we went on the trip to the castle, Thornton called me one night on my cell phone and asked me if I wanted to go with him and some other people to the movie theater. I asked him who was going, and he told me it would be himself, Marshall, and Martinez.

As soon as he said Martinez, I told him I would rather not go. After spending the last few months with Martinez, I was more annoyed by him than anything. He seemed to always drag the group down, and a lot of the time, he was just annoying and had to be the center of attention. Sometimes, I would catch myself rolling my eyes when he was telling us stories about things he did before the military that I didn't think were true. Half the time he would try to get me to go out with him, and I always said no, and that got annoying after a while too. We stayed friends and still spent time together, but I tried to keep my distance from him over the next few weeks. I felt I had a closer relationship with Marshall and Thornton, and I preferred spending time with them.

Weeks went by and the four of us continued to spend a lot of time together at work and after. One day after work, a group of us were hanging out in Martinez's room in the barracks. I was sitting on a beanbag chair and watching Martinez do stuff around his room, and I am not sure what changed in him that day or what changed in me, but I looked at him and thought he looked different.

I suddenly noticed features of him I had never noticed before. Matt was more handsome than I had remembered thinking. He was walking around his room without a shirt on, which was not the first time I had seen him without a shirt, but that day I looked at his body and noticed the muscles on his arms, shoulders and abs. He had always looked that way, but I had never found him attractive in that way before that day. Still, he looked strong and muscular, and I went from viewing him as a skinny boy to suddenly looking at him as a man.

I looked at him and asked him how he got so tan.

He just looked at me and laughed and said, "Because I am Mexican."

I felt stupid because, obviously, that was why he was so tan. My face flushed, and I quickly changed the subject because I could tell that he saw I was staring at him, and he seemed way too satisfied with himself. I turned my attention to something else and started talking to one of my other friends while Martinez kept walking around his room, putting things away and organizing.

The next weekend, we all sat in one of the lounge rooms in the barracks and drank and played cards. Martinez had been flirting with me as he usually did, and I wasn't as mean to him as I normally was. I didn't flirt with him, but I also didn't shut him down when he started flirting like I normally did.

I could tell he was drunk, and I started to feel that way, too. He looked into my eyes and held eye contact for a few seconds before he asked if he could kiss me.

At that moment, I had a feeling I hadn't had before. I wanted him to kiss me, and I had no idea why suddenly I felt that way.

"Yea, you can kiss me," I said playfully.

He leaned forward to me and put his lips against mine. I felt lightheaded when his lips touched mine, and my stomach started fluttering. It was a great first kiss. He pulled away just for a moment before leaning in and kissing me again.

I think back on that night, and I still am unsure of what came over me. From that night forward, we were inseparable. Once I put my guard down enough to let myself fall for him, I fell hard.

By this time, we had been friends for about eight months. He had grown on me. Eight months didn't seem like a very long time, but we spent almost every day together. We worked together, hung out after work together, and when I thought about it, I realized I had spent a lot of time with him.

He was obsessed with running, and I needed the work, so in the weeks leading up to the night we kissed, I would join him. I had moments where I didn't want to be around him at all, but then other times, I enjoyed being around him. Part of me was afraid of him leaving and finding someone else or just forgetting about me, and I had feelings for him, even though I was confused by what the feelings meant. It was amazing when we had fun and grew closer together, but some things still bothered me about him.

I had never had the feelings that I felt for Matt during those first couple of weeks that we dated. Matt was romantic, loving, and sweet. He loved to hold me and be near me.

He finally left for his detachment a couple of weeks later, and after that, nothing was the same between us.

I knew I would not see him for three months, and it would likely be at least a month before I even heard from him. It was hard on me, but I did it to myself because I started that relationship knowing he was leaving for three months.

I was emotional the night he left, but I had my friends there with me. They made it a lot easier for me to get through the three months Matt was gone. The first month was long, but I kept busy with all the things I normally did before I started dating him.

It was just over a month before I got my first letter from him. He was sweet, and he talked about how much he missed me and couldn't wait to see me again.

He told me about where he had been and what it was like being on the ship. At the end of the letter, he said something that hurt me, though. Matt said he had a lot of opportunities to do wrong by me, but he didn't and wouldn't do anything to hurt me.

I knew he was on the ship with women and men, and many women were in the Navy, so there were many people he was with that he had never met before. I assumed he would make new friends, but I never thought that he would be pursued by anyone sexually or that he would pursue anyone. But once I read that, the thought was in my head.

I could not shake it.

I let it go, and we continued our long-distance relationship over the next two months until the detachment returned to Okinawa.

One night, he surprised me by coming to my barracks room before I knew he would be back. I jumped into his arms and gave him an enormous hug. He picked me up and spun me around before he kissed me. Once he came back, we were both so excited to see each other again and be able to hold and kiss one another.

We hung out for a couple of hours, and he told me everything about his detachment. I got him up-to-speed on what he had missed while he was gone, but it wasn't much. I could tell as he talked he had more confidence in himself and had made a lot of new friends with other Marines in our barracks.

Over the next few days, he started hanging out more with his friends he had met on the ship. Some of them were women, and it wouldn't have bothered me as much if he wasn't so openly flirtatious with them in front of me. I had never been the jealous type, but I also didn't like that he showed more interest in some of the other women than he did me. They had developed friendships being stuck on a ship together for three months, and I tried to not let it bother me. It didn't take more than a couple of weeks before he started ditching me to go hang out with girls he was on the ship with.

One morning, a few days after Matt was back, I was showering in my barracks bathroom. Matt had stayed in my room the night before since we had been apart for a few months. I was in the shower, and out of nowhere, Matt pulled back the curtain and got in the shower with me.

My first initial reaction was panic. I don't know why that was my first reaction, but Cain's face came to me at that moment. After joining the military, I still thought about my birth family and some of my foster families often. None of the memories went away, but I was so busy with my new life that the memories weren't so persistent.

I pushed the thought aside and asked Matt what he was doing. He seemed confused by the question and said he figured he would take a shower with me.

I felt exposed and uncomfortable in a way I had never felt with Matt before. I had never been in a shower with someone before and I thought maybe that was why I felt uneasy. Even though I had no memory of Cain doing anything to me in the shower, I couldn't get rid of the overwhelming anxiousness I felt and the image of Cain in my mind.

A few weeks after Matt came back from the detachment, I broke up with him. He had never done anything wrong in particular, but there was something off between us and I realized I didn't want to be in a relationship. After we broke up, we still spent a lot of time together because we had a lot of the same friends. Our original friend group never changed, so we didn't have a lot of options but to hang out together, and we fell back into our friendship even though we had ended our romantic relationship.

We had been broken up for a couple of weeks and our friendship was going really good. We had talked about dating each other again on a few occasions, but I told him I needed time. A few days later, Matt officially asked me if I wanted to go out with him again.

"I don't know what I want," I said.

"I'm not going to wait around forever, Sheila. You need to decide, or I am going to move on."

"I just need to think about it," I told him.

A couple of days later, I made up my mind and told Matt that I thought we should start dating again. I struggled to imagine him not in my life and that finally helped me come to a decision. I hoped things would work out along the way. Our relationship never got better, though. We stayed together, but it seemed like there were a lot of ups and downs in our relationship. We had a lot of fun together but it wasn't great all of the time.

Our relationship never got better, though. We stayed together, but it seemed like there were a lot of ups and downs in our relationship. We had a lot of fun together, but it wasn't great all the time.

We had started dating in September 2008, so I was excited when February came the following year, since it would be our first Valentine's Day together. I had made hints to him for weeks prior to Valentine's Day about getting engaged and getting married. Still, we never talked about it in depth.

When I joined the military, I didn't exactly have my life planned out. Back then, I had decided I wasn't going to have kids, and I would probably never get married. All of that changed after I started dating Matt, though.

I started thinking about having kids and having a family, but I also was terrified of being a mother. All I knew is that if I was ever going to have kids, I would need to be married first and I guess that's why the idea of getting married to Matt came into my mind.

On Valentine's Day, he came to my barracks room and gave me my gifts. He had gotten me a stuffed animal, a card, and a jewelry box with a necklace inside. He told me to put the necklace on, so I took it out of the box to hand it to him to help me put it on, and he grabbed my hand, and put a diamond ring on my ring finger.

"Will you marry me?"

I was in shock and disbelief that he had just asked me to marry him.

Excitedly, I said, "Yes!"

Please, God, let this be real.

I was on track to having a normal life; the way it was always supposed to be.

A few days later, we both called home and told our families. My parents knew I had been dating Matt for a few months, and they knew we had been friends for a while prior to us dating. I think both of my parents thought it was a huge mistake, but they never said that when I told them. They were both happy for me and my mom got right to work planning our wedding.

I don't know if I was in love in the way I should have been to decide to marry someone. I was more in love with the idea of being in love and being engaged and married. If I was ever going to have kids, I knew I wanted to have them when I was still young. If I ever did have kids, I had to be married first. I didn't want to disappoint my parents by having a child outside of marriage. Also, didn't want to be like Beverly, and I knew she had a lot of kids without being married.

I had no way to measure my relationship with Matt since I had nothing to compare it to. I don't think I had a clue what love was or what it was supposed to feel like. My feelings for Matt were intense, but I didn't know if that was enough to commit to a lifetime of being together.

We both would leave Japan in 2010 to head to our new duty stations, and if we didn't get married, we had no guarantee we would be stationed together.

Right after we got engaged, my Sergeant sent me back to the States in Arizona on a detachment.

He had told me when he picked me for the detachment; he thought it would be good for me to get away from Matt for a little while.

None of the Marines I worked with were thrilled about me dating Matt or getting engaged to him. Shia told me I wasn't thinking clearly, and that I was making a mistake. He knew we had such a hot and cold relationship with one another, and he didn't want to see me rush into anything. I didn't listen to him, though.

I returned to Okinawa after the two-month detachment ended, and we ended up getting married in a courthouse off base in Ginowan City, Japan. My biggest reason for rushing into the marriage was the fear of being separated from Matt. After getting married in June at the courthouse, things started getting rough in our relationship. We started fighting a lot more and getting into more physical fights.

A lot of my frustration was with the way he spent his money and how much he spent on drinking every weekend. We had been saving up for our wedding, and it ended up being mostly me paying for the wedding. From the time we got engaged to the time we went home for our wedding, I had saved up and spent over $16,000 on our wedding.

When it came time to leave Okinawa to head back to the states for our wedding, Matt and I were thrilled to be having our wedding and to be back home in the states. Despite the issues in our relationship, we both felt a sense of anticipation and excitement as we boarded the plane to head back to the states. After the fourteen hour flight, we finally landed at the Airport and after as we came down the escalator to head to the baggage claim, I saw my parents and brothers waiting for us.

When I went on the Detachment to Arizona earlier that year, my family drove to Arizona to visit me for a couple of days, but I did not get as much time with them as I had hoped to. It had been about seven months since I last saw them and I could feel the excitement boiling up in me as I approached them. Jax and John ran up to me and wrapped their arms around me.

I gave both of them kisses. "I missed you so much!"

I stood up and turned to Matt to introduce him to my family. "These are my little brothers, Jax, John, and Michael."

"Mom, Dad, this is Matt." Matt extended his arm and shook both of my parents' hands after he said hi to my brothers.

"I am so happy to finally meet all of you," Matt said.

As we walked to grab our bags, my brothers started talking to Matt about anything that came to mind. After, we headed to my parents' van, and they drove us back to their house where we would stay during our trip.

We were only home for a couple of days before the wedding, so all the last minute wedding prep happened quickly.

Before I knew it, I was in the church with my dad's arm around mine as he walked me down the aisle to Matt. I was happy, excited, and nervous. My entire body shook from the nerves the entire walk down the aisle. My heart raced as I faced the crowd and felt their eyes on me. I smiled as we slowly walked past the pews with the guests and I could feel my mouth quivering as I tried to hold my smile. I had never felt so nervous in my life, and I had never felt my body shaking from nerves like that before, either.

It was a beautiful ceremony though, and it was over before I really had time to process anything or calm down. The reception followed right after. Matt and I got into a couple of arguments during the reception because of his family. I don't remember now why we were even fighting, but I felt like he was pushing me away. After our wedding day, things calmed down between us and we got excited about heading out for our honeymoon. When we left a couple of days later, it was hard to say goodbye to my family, but I felt excited about starting our honeymoon.

We stepped out of the airport and into the humid Hawaiian air. The salty scent of the ocean wafted towards us, and I closed my eyes, taking a deep breath. The sun beat down on my face, and I squinted up at the sky, feeling the warmth on my skin. It was a stark contrast to the cold weather we had just left in Ohio.

As we rode in the taxi to our hotel, I couldn't take my eyes off of the landscape all around us. The lush greenery and towering mountains surrounded us, and I couldn't believe how beautiful it was. The hotel was just a stone's throw away from the beach, and as we walked into our room, I could hear the gentle sound of waves crashing against the shore.

Matt and I spent the next few days exploring the island and enjoying each other's company.

On the second day of our honeymoon, I started feeling lightheaded and nauseous. At first, I brushed it off as jet lag or the heat, but the symptoms persisted.

One afternoon, we stumbled upon a convenience store that sold pregnancy tests. My heart raced as I picked one up so I could check just to be sure I wasn't pregnant. After we bought it, we headed back to our hotel room. I took the test, my hands shaking, and watched as two blue lines appeared.

I was pregnant.

The next morning, Matt and I wanted to find a payphone so we could call his family and tell them the news. We got ready and headed out on our search.

The weather was gorgeous, and I wore a light beach dress over my swimsuit since we were planning to head to the beach later. I was still feeling very nauseous and at times I would get extremely lightheaded and have to stop to make sure I didn't lose my balance. I felt like I had vertigo and I could not get that feeling to stop.

The humid air hit me as we stepped out onto the sidewalk. I could smell the ocean water mixed with sand, and despite feeling nauseous still, I was in paradise. Hawaii was a lot like Okinawa, but there was more of a tropical feel in Hawaii.

We walked for a little while and talked about how we were going to break the news to our families. Finally, we found a payphone and Matt called his mom. As he spoke to her, I waited anxiously, unsure of how my own parents would react to the news. *Would they be disappointed that I had gotten pregnant so soon? Would they be angry that I hadn't waited until we were more settled?*

After spending five days in Hawaii, it was time to head back to Okinawa. When we returned to Japan, I wasted no time in making an appointment at the medical center on base to get checked out.

The doctor confirmed what I already suspected: I was pregnant. But what I didn't expect was to find out that I was already eight weeks along. The news was both exhilarating and terrifying. I couldn't believe how much my life had changed in such a short amount of time, and I had no idea how I was going to navigate this new chapter of my life. But one thing was for sure: I was determined to do everything in my power to give my baby the best life possible.

My body was changing at an alarming rate as I entered my fifth month of pregnancy. I knew I wasn't as attractive as I used to be, but I never expected the brutal honesty that came from Matt's lips one day.

He told me he wasn't attracted to me anymore because of my weight gain. His words cut me like a knife, and I struggled to comprehend how he could be so callous.

The next day, I was in my room with Matt talking. I traced my fingertips over my swollen belly, feeling the life growing inside of me. Matt's rejection of my changing body hurt more than I could express.

He looked at me with disappointment and disgust, and the warmth in his gaze had turned colder each day. One day, he muttered something hurtful under his breath, and before I knew it, my hand flew across his cheek. His eyes darted toward me angrily, and without a word, he stormed out of my room.

Feeling guilty, I went to find him in his barracks room. I wanted to know what was going on with him and why he was being so mean. But when I confronted him, he exploded. He yelled at me for slapping him, and I yelled back that I barely even touched him. Suddenly, he slapped me across the face, mimicking my earlier slap.

"You think you can hit me and get away with it?" he spat, his fingers digging into my arms. "I'll show you what happens when you put your hands on me."

I sobbed, feeling helpless and trapped, until suddenly Marshall was there, pulling Matt off of me. I stumbled backwards, shaking with fear and pain, as Marshall helped me to my feet.

He held me as I cried, telling me it wasn't my fault. He said that no one deserved to be treated like that. But the guilt gnawed at me. *If I hadn't slapped him first, maybe this wouldn't have happened.*

My body shook and my eyes filled with tears as I walked out of the room. I didn't know what had happened, how things had escalated so quickly. I was so surprised by my behavior, I could not understand why I had become so furious that I had to resort to slapping him. *Why the hell did you slap him, Sheila?*

I had this sickening feeling in my gut as I thought of my birth mother and father and imagined what their fights were like. I didn't need much of an imagination to realize that they were probably very similar to what I just went through. After everything I had done to get myself to this point, I was scared to death that I had grown up to be Beverly and somehow managed to marry a man who was exactly like Victor.

This can't be real. I need to fix this and make it right.

Our relationship was never the same. It was a constant battle of physical and verbal abuse on both sides. After we left Japan a couple of months later, we went to Jacksonville, North Carolina. Things were better for a little while after we got there. We stayed in a hotel for almost the first month because there was no housing on base, and we were house hunting, looking for a rental that would be good for us and our baby.

We found the perfect house, and it was out in the country, a little way from town. The layout was so open and spacious. The house had that perfect natural lighting. We moved in a couple of weeks later, and we started making the house our own, and I think that was something we both needed. It was something we both had waited for so long to have. We needed a home of our own to have our own space and time together.

When things were good, we had a lot of fun together. Playing video games was something we really enjoyed doing, and we would often have our friends over to hang out and have a game night. We had a shared love for movies, with a lot of overlap in what we liked to watch, and the same went for our music taste. We had a great time watching movies or listening to music and just being together. I loved to cook, but I did not know how to cook any authentic Mexican dishes. Matt stepped right in to teach me how to cook meals he loved. We had a lot of fun together, but we had just as many fights and arguments. When he was sweet and loving, he made me feel like the only person in the world who mattered to him, but those moments were growing scarcer.

When I was eight months pregnant, we had a disagreement just before we were both getting ready to step into the shower together.

The water was already running in the shower, steam filling the bathroom and bedroom as Matt and I stood on opposite sides of the bedroom. Our argument had escalated quickly, and now we were both seething with anger. I could feel my heart pounding in my chest as I looked at him, his face fuming. I turned and started to walk away to go to the other bathroom outside of our bedroom.

"I'm showering in the other bedroom," I muttered.

Matt lunged at me, grabbing my arm so tightly it hurt.

"Let go of me!" I screamed, struggling to break free.

But he wouldn't release his grip, and I felt a surge of panic rising in my chest. I tried to pull away, but he was too strong, dragging me across the floor towards the bathroom. My naked body scraped against the carpet as I kicked and thrashed, desperate to escape.

Finally, he let go of my foot, and I rolled over, gasping for air. Tears streamed down my face as I watched him walk away. I could still feel his hands on my skin, and his fingers digging into my flesh. I was terrified of what might happen next.

I couldn't imagine him ever hurting me, but at the same time, I wasn't sure what he was capable of.

Every ounce of the young man I had met two years ago in Okinawa was gone. I didn't even know who this person was anymore.

Even worse, I didn't know who I was anymore.

I wasn't a fighter, and I had never been the type of person to fight like this. He got infuriated and got physical with me, and in turn, I did the same.

He would get so livid, and sometimes he would charge toward me like he was going to hit me. Once I saw a certain look in his eyes, I would run away and lock myself in a room or closet away from him.

One time, sitting in a closet waiting for Matt to calm down, I looked down at my enormous belly and silently cried.

My mind went back to all of those times as a little girl that I hid in closets, and I hated myself so much at that moment.

I couldn't believe that my life had gotten to this point. I thought I had escaped everything about my childhood that scared me, and here I was living through those moments all over again.

It was a vicious cycle, and I didn't know how I was going to get out.

CHAPTER 14

I was induced to give birth to our son, Quentin, at 7 o'clock in the morning on July 18th, 2010. We drove to the hospital, and my mind raced with a mix of emotions - anticipation, fear, and excitement. The doctors had estimated that Quentin would be over nine pounds, and his size, coupled with my high blood pressure, caused them to decide it was best to induce me rather than wait for my due date. After getting to the hospital and getting to the delivery room, the nurses started the process. It took hours until I dilated enough for the nurses to break my water. Once the Pitocin started working, the contractions came, but I wasn't able to start pushing until later in the evening.

I waited impatiently for signs that Quentin was ready to make his grand entrance. But the labor seemed to drag on endlessly and I was exhausted and my entire body was in pain. The contractions were coming fast and strong, but my body just wouldn't cooperate. It took what felt like an eternity before I dilated to 10 cm. I felt a wave of fear wash over me as I was told it was time to push. No amount of preparation could have prepared me for the intense sensation of pressure and pain that flooded through my body with every push. I pushed and pushed, but it didn't feel like anything was happening and for a long time, there was no progress. After I had pushed for two hours, the nurses could finally see Quentin's head crowning, and I thought that was a sign that I was close to the end.

For three long hours, I pushed with everything I had. I took brief breaks, trying to catch my breath and find the strength to push again. After the first two hours, the nurses started having me get in different positions and push, in the hopes that if I was in a different position, I would be able to push my baby out. Despite my best efforts, I couldn't make any progress. I felt defeated, exhausted, and scared.

The nurse said she could see the baby's head, but his hands were up next to his head, resting against his cheeks. The nurse told me she was worried my baby was stuck and if I could not push him out soon, then I would have to go into surgery.

They had me push for a little longer, and when the three-hour mark came, they said they could no longer let me continue, and I had to have a C-Section. I let out a deep sigh of relief when I realized I didn't have to push anymore. After so much agony and effort up to that point, I couldn't believe I would ever have mustered up the strength to push him out.

The nurses carefully moved me onto the gurney, and the wheels squeaked in the hallway as they took me to the operating room. The nurses moved quickly, but carefully transferring me to the operating table, the sheets cool against my skin. I had been there for hours and the painkillers had left me feeling drained and lethargic. It was such an effort to keep my eyes open during the surgery that I barely managed to stay awake.

When I opened my eyes, I saw the doctor and then closed them again. *I want to fall asleep. I'm so tired right now.* My eyes opened again, and the doctor talked for a minute, but I couldn't process anything. I was too tired to think, and I wanted it all to be over.

Over the next 15 or 20 minutes, I continued to doze off and then suddenly wake up and open my eyes until they finally pulled my son from my abdomen. The nurse carefully carried Quentin over to me, wrapped in a sheet, and I could hear the faint sound of his breathing. I couldn't hold Quentin yet because I was still in surgery and I am not sure I would have been able to hold him, anyway. Matt followed close behind as they took Quentin out of the room.

After the doctor put me back together, I was rolled into another room for recovery. I had to lie there for two hours, my mind racing as I stared up at the ceiling. The room was still and quiet, occupied by a few other patients, each one resting peacefully in their beds. I felt paralyzed from the waist down, and the only thing I could do was stare up at the ceiling until I drifted off into sleep. A nurse came and checked on me a couple of times, assessed my incision, asked me how I was feeling, and then she left.

After two hours had passed, a nurse finally returned, and they awoke me to be informed that they were prepared to take me to the room where I could meet my son. After all the waiting and anticipation, I was overwhelmed with joy at the feeling of being able to hold him for the first time.

When I gazed down at my newborn son, my heart was filled with an immense amount of love and joy. It felt like an unbelievable dream to be holding my newborn baby in my arms for the first time.

The feeling I had when my little brothers were born, I thought it would be the same feeling when I had my own child. I was able to recall the warm feeling of joy that rushed through me when I first held them in my arms after their births. When I had my own child, I expected to feel the same as before, but the overwhelming love I felt was indescribable. I studied my son's face, feeling the softness of his skin and admiring each feature, and thought that he was the most perfect baby I had ever seen.

I think back to that day sometimes and relive that moment. It makes my heart ache when I remember that first moment of holding him and how quickly he turned into the young man that he has grown into. Sometimes, I go back to that moment and live through it again in my head so I can feel the complete happiness that I felt in those first moments when I held my son. I look at him now and see him becoming a man. He is such a passionate, confident, outspoken young man. I remembered holding him as a baby in those first moments and never imagined for a second he would grow into the person he is today.

It is hard sometimes for me to remember him being so tiny and how he snuggled on my chest when he was sleepy and would wrap his tiny hands around my fingers to hold on to me or rest his hands on my face as he slept to feel my skin.

Those moments made being a mother so worth it.

I see this same boy now who has turned into a pre-teen. He has an attitude and a mind of his own, and it was so hard for me to wrap my head around when he grew up.

The next morning, as I held Quentin in my arms, I couldn't help but try to imagine what it was like for Beverly as she held her babies for the first time. I wondered if she even had the same feelings that I had when I held Quentin for the first time. I thought about how it would have been for her when Damien was born and she held her first son in her arms. *Did she feel the undying love that I feel for Quentin? When she held me in her arms for the first time, did she feel any love for me? Maybe, by then, giving birth was just another day for her. And maybe it had been that way for her even before I was born.*

As much as I tried, I couldn't imagine how someone could hold their infant in their arms after giving birth and not feel the love that was in my heart in those first moments I held Quentin. Even hours later and the exhaustion set in, I still couldn't understand how someone could not care about their children enough to want to give them all the love they had. And maybe that was part of the problem. I did not know her then, but maybe she had nothing to give to us.

My connection with Quentin's father, Matt, diminished quickly following his birth. Quentin was a very colicky baby, and his cries had a piercing, high-pitched sound. Once the initial rush of bringing home a newborn had worn off, Matt saw Quentin as a chore and a burden. Whenever I asked him to help with Quentin, I was greeted with a cold, unwelcoming attitude. It got to the point where it was easier to take care of everything myself instead of asking Matt for help. His attitude got worse every day, and he made me feel like I was an incompetent mother because I would ask him if he could change Quentin's diaper or hold him when he was crying. We were both still in the military, and after my maternity leave, I had to return to work full time.

We were in the same department, and we both worked the same hours, so we were equally tired by the end of the day. I felt the strain of having to shoulder the responsibility of caring for Quentin alone.

It didn't matter what I was doing. If Quentin was crying and needed something, I would call Matt's name, but he'd still be glued to the t.v. or video games. I'd have to abandon what I was doing and take care of Quentin myself.

Matt was content letting him cry. As Quentin got older, if Matt held him while he was crying, Matt would get so frustrated. He would start rocking him aggressively in his arms, thinking that would help, but it never calmed Quentin down and it would scare me when I could see Matt's anger was getting the best of him. I wanted to protect Quentin from Matt, who I feared could not contain his anger and might accidentally hurt him.

Our relationship continued to decline over the next year. The same month Quentin turned a year old, I decided to EAS (End of Active Service) and leave the military instead of re-enlisting. Matt had a month in the service after I was done with the military until he could EAS unless he decided to re-enlist. I tried encouraging him to re-enlist, but he didn't want to.

We had broken up earlier that year, and I had moved out. About a month after I moved out of our house and into an apartment, Matt moved in with me. Our lease was up with our house and he could not afford to stay there on his own and one day he came to my apartment and told me he had nowhere to go.

Eventually, we started working on things again, but I did not have faith it would work. It didn't take more than a couple of weeks before I caught him cheating on me. I didn't do anything about it, though. We fought the day I found out, but I didn't know what to do, and I had just let him move in with me. I tried to let it go and move on, and he promised that he would work on himself and try to change for me and for Quentin.

After Matt left the service, he wanted us to both move to Texas and live there, and my gut told me I shouldn't do it. When we had decided to get married, we discussed where we would live if we both left the military and we had decided that Ohio made the most sense. Now that it was actually time to make that move, it surprised me that he wanted to go back to Texas.

I had my dad come down to North Carolina and help me drive a U-Haul back to Ohio with all of our stuff. I headed back to Ohio to get things situated while Matt visited his family in Texas.

He planned to be down there for two weeks.

But two weeks turned into four weeks, and each week he got harder and harder to contact. Occasionally, Matt would answer the phone, but rarely.

When we talked, I would ask him when he was coming back to Ohio so we could start looking for a place.

I wanted him back to be with me and Quentin.

He kept saying soon, but I could never get an actual answer out of him. Matt said his mom was going through a lot, and she needed him there, so I tried to be understanding and let it go.

Matt went down to Texas to see his family in August. Finally, in October, he told me he would need more time down there. I pleaded with him to fly back up to Ohio for a few days to visit me and Quentin, but he couldn't afford a plane ticket. I purchased a two-way ticket for him, but in the back of my mind, I hoped that when he returned, the feeling of home would be too strong for him to leave.

I was able to find a hotel that was close to the area where his father's relatives were living. We left my parents' house and drove to the airport to pick up Matt. Once we saw Matt at the airport, I set Quentin down so he could run to his dad, but Quentin didn't leave my side. I felt a slight sense of panic when Quentin didn't seem to recognize his dad and did not react to him. It was obvious that it bothered Matt, and over the next couple of days, he acted as if there wasn't a connection between him and Quentin. I could tell Matt was happy to see him, but I knew that was it.

There wasn't enough attachment there for him to desire not to leave again.

As Matt's departure came closer, desperation set in.

We stayed at his aunt's place for the last night, but sleep was elusive. His uncle had offered him a ride to Texas the next day, and I couldn't bear the thought of him leaving again. I pleaded and begged, telling him I needed him with me, that our son needed him too. But he had his reasons, the same ones as before. The car and some of his belongings were down in Texas, and he kept saying he couldn't just leave them behind. He said that his mom still needed him, too.

I tried to assure him we could sort it out later, that the car was mine anyway, but he wouldn't listen. All I wanted was for him to stay a little longer, to give us a chance to work things out. But it seemed like nothing could change his mind.

That night, as we lay in bed, I could barely bring myself to close my eyes. Matt woke me up at four in the morning to say goodbye before he and his cousin hit the road. I watched him leave, feeling a sense of hopelessness wash over me.

The rest of the morning was a blur. Breakfast with his family, packing up our things, and heading back to my parent's place with Quentin.

I couldn't stop the tears from falling during the two-hour drive. It felt like my world was crashing down around me.

I was more embarrassed than anything else that I had to go back home alone and face my parents.

My parents were already upset that I went to see him, and they told me it was a bad idea. They knew I would try to get him to stay, but they did not think he would, and they were right.

I didn't see Quentin's dad again until almost two years later, when we had the final hearing for our divorce.

SHEILA RUBY

CHAPTER 15

Right after Christmas, a couple of months after Matt came to Ohio to visit, I moved in with my best friend from high school. Shelly lived in the country with daughter, and she talked me into moving in with her. It was just the four of us- me, Shelly, and our two kids. She had a daughter who was a year older than Quentin.

At the end of January, we invited some friends over on a Saturday night to play cards. Shelly had talked me into messaging a guy from high school a couple of weeks earlier. He and I had been chatting on and off during the last week, and I decided to invite him over that night to hang out and play cards.

I had known Joe since high school, even though he was two years younger than me. During my Junior and Senior years in school, I took classes with him and I had a crush on him. As we messaged each other, I found out that he had a son as well, who was a year older than Quentin.

That night, I asked him to come over and hang out and Joe said he didn't have his son, so he was free. Joe came over to Shelly's house and hung out with us and a couple of other people we went to school with.

When Joe walked inside, I noticed right away that he looked a lot different. I stood there looking at him, unable to believe it had been four years since the last time I had seen him. He had aged, but the warmth of his smile was still as comforting as I remembered.

We played cards for a couple of hours, and we all drank and made conversation. It was getting late and the other people we had over had to leave. Shelly picked up a bit and then let Joe and I know she was heading to bed.

Instead of staying in the dining room, Joe and I moved to the living room and sat on the couch for a couple of hours talking and playing Trivia Pursuit to pass the time. We joked around and playfully flirted on and off. We had a great time talking and laughing, but eventually it was time for him to leave.

I walked him to the door, and Joe turned and wrapped his arms around me, hugging me before he left. He held me close for a moment, and I could feel his heart racing against my chest. We separated and Joe smiled and said goodbye again as he walked out the door.

A couple of minutes later, I got a message from Joe. "I had a really good time hanging out with you."

I was so happy to get that message, and I had a feeling I would see him again.

The next day we kept talking to each other, sending messages to one another. Later that night, Joe said he was at his parents' house watching a movie and invited me over to hang out with him.

I asked Shelly if she would watch Quentin for me so I could hang out with Joe.

"Absolutely! Go have a good time, and I will watch Quentin."

"Thank you so much! I really appreciate you watching him for me," I said.

Shelly was excited that Joe and I hit it off and that we wanted to see each other again.

I drove to Joe's parents' house, since that was where he was living at the time. He greeted me at the door when I got there, and asked me to be quiet since his parents were sleeping already. He grabbed my hand and led me down to their basement to watch a movie.

We sat down and talked for a little while. Joe asked me if I wanted to smoke weed, and I said yes, so he grabbed his dugout, and we did a couple of one-hits before he started another movie since the first movie he was watching was over already.

We didn't watch much of the movie, and the next morning, I couldn't remember what movie he had even put on. We talked for a long time and then curled up on the couch under the blankets and cuddle since it had gotten really cold. After a few minutes, we started kissing and then one thing led to another.

Joe woke me up around 4:00 a.m. gently shaking me and whispering my name. I woke up and felt disoriented and exhausted. Joe told me that his dad had just yelled down and said his mom needed to leave for work soon and my car was parked behind hers.

Since I hadn't planned on staying the night, I got my stuff around and Joe walked me upstairs to the door to say goodbye to me. Joe hugged me and gave me a kiss before I walked out the door and said goodbye. As I walked to my car, I could see that Joe's dad was already in his truck, letting it warm up, and I felt so embarrassed that he found out that I was there that way.

After that day, Joe and I talked every day, and came to see me a couple of times a week. He finally met Quentin and started spending time with Quentin as well, since I had Quentin all the time. It took a little longer for me to meet Joe's son, Cole, but it was only maybe a couple of weeks after he first met Quentin before he took me back to his parents' house to meet his parents and his son.

I will never forget the first time I met his son. He was this little two and a half year old boy with long brown hair that was very curly on the ends. He had the chubbiest cheeks and the biggest brown eyes I had ever seen.

The first thing he said to me was, "Girl, make me food!"

I laughed but didn't know how to respond. I was shocked at how well he spoke and wasn't expecting it because my son was only a year younger and was still non-verbal. Joe laughed too, but told his son Cole to be nice and go ask his grandma to get him food if he wanted something to eat. We only stayed at his parents' house for a little while, and then I left to go back home.

The next week, we had our boys meet each other and took the kids somewhere for a playdate. I had to drive and pay for everything since Joe wasn't working at the time, but that didn't bother me because I liked him.

I felt like we had a good connection. We went out for the playdate, and the boys got along well. Quentin did great with Joe and Cole did great with me, so I think we both felt that things might be able to keep moving forward.

Joe and I continued to see each other regularly and talked every day over the next couple of months.

One night, I got a text from Joe that said *'ILY'*.

I showed the text to my friend Shelly because I wasn't sure what it meant, and she said that he meant *'I love you'*.

I showed the text to my friend Shelly because I wasn't sure what it meant, and she said that he meant "I love you."

I didn't know what to say, so I just ignored the text and acted like I didn't know what it meant.

A couple of days later, Joe and I were talking over the phone. Before he hung up, he paused for a moment, then said, "I love you."

"I love you too," I said back to him.

I was nervous about falling in love with someone.

Joe knew how much Matt had hurt me. He knew that my heart had been broken, but Joe promised he wouldn't do the same. He assured me he would never do anything to cause me pain.

It didn't take long for the rest of our relationship to progress. As we spent more time together, Joe and I grew closer. We had long conversations about everything and anything, and I found myself thinking about him even when we weren't together. We talked every day and tried to see each other as much as we could.

One of the first things he would say to me when he saw me or talked to me was, "Did I tell you that you're beautiful today?"

I would smile and respond, "No, not yet."

"You're beautiful, Sheila," he would say with complete sincerity.

The realization hit me that I was falling in love with him. I loved that we could share our dreams and aspirations with one another. It was as if we had found something truly special in each other, and we knew we didn't want to let it go.

My best friend Shelly started getting frustrated that I was spending all of my time with Joe, and one night she had even made a comment that she felt like Joe was changing me. Shelly got sick of me being gone all the time. She told me she felt like I was barely living with her, and she asked me to move out. I was hurt and so outraged that she would do something like that to me, but I didn't know how to respond. I was so wrapped up in Joe that I hadn't thought about Shelly at all.

After I told Joe what happened, he told me to come stay with him at his parents' house. I didn't want to move into Joe's parents, but I knew it was that or go back to my parents' house. The thought of having to move back in with my parents gave me anxiety. I moved all of my stuff to Joe's parents' house, and they said that we had a month to find our own place.

Joe and I started searching for a rental. We had been dating for four months and Joe still didn't have a job. He was determined to find work so that we could manage to rent a place.

We ended up finding a house for rent in the same town, but I didn't have the money up front for a down payment and the first month's rent. Joe talked me into asking my grandparents for money, and they, of course, gave me the money I needed. They gave us the conditions when we went to their house to get the money the day we needed to pay the landlord and told us how much time we had to pay them back.

I was able to get the house that Joe and I had found. I took the money that my grandparents had lent to me and paid it to the landlord and signed the lease. Joe and I started moving into our new home together shortly after that.

My grandparents gave us some furniture they didn't need anymore, and Joe's parents gave us some items for the house as well. Over the next couple of months, Joe started bringing more of his stuff from his parents' house into our new home. After a while, it started to feel like a home. It wasn't much, but it was ours, and it was filled equally with both of our life belongings. I loved everything about that house.

The day that house burned down, I stood there watching and wondering how I could move forward after this. I had no idea how I would rebuild a home for my family after losing everything so suddenly.

I was in shock for days after the house fire, and none of it seemed real at all. I couldn't believe I had lost everything. At the same time, I had this odd sense of relief that maybe I could start over and really have a fresh start to my life without bringing along any of the baggage I had before.

Unfortunately, I wouldn't be getting the fresh start that I thought I would be getting.

After the house fire, we started staying in my parents' camper that they had parked in their driveway since we did not have anywhere to go. My parents couldn't fit all of us in their house. It was difficult living out of the camper, and I think living in that situation caused more issues in my relationship with Joe.

One of my good friends at the time would invite us all over to her house quite a bit, so we would at least have the chance to get out of the camper and not feel so cooped up together.

My friend started acting strange around Joe after about a month, and I picked up on it right away. I didn't think too much of it, though. Living in the camper, Joe and I started arguing a lot more, and he often brought up the house burning down, and blamed me for him losing everything. Once I found out how much I was getting back from my insurance company, I realized I could probably use that money to get a start on my own without Joe.

When Joe was at work one day, I packed up all of his stuff in bags, and when he came back to the camper after work, I told him it wasn't working out and I wanted him to go. He made it obvious he no longer wanted to pursue a relationship with me, so I decided it would be best to end things right then. Joe was livid and, in a rush, he gathered his things and got into his car and drove away.

I started crying because we were fighting and yelling at each other before he left. Before he left, I kept telling him he made it clear he didn't want to be with me. He said that it was all in my head, and he couldn't believe I was doing this. I told him we could talk through it, but he was too upset, so he left. It was maybe fifteen minutes after he left when my friend showed up at the camper.

She walked in the door and looked around and asked, "Where is all of Joe's stuff?"

The question confused me because there were no obvious signs that his stuff was gone. We just had a house fire, so the only things we even had were clothes, but none of our clothes were even out. I told her I packed up Joe's stuff, and he left, and she gave me a shocked look, but I could tell that she already knew.

I instantly got a sinking feeling in my gut that there was something going on between her and Joe.

I talked to her for a few minutes and told her about the fight we had. She said she was just stopping by since she had a few minutes, but she had to head home. After a few minutes, I drove out to Joe's parents' house because I knew that was the only place he would go.

I got to Joe's parents' house, and when he was not there.

I had a feeling I knew where he was.

Part of me didn't want to believe it, so I got out of the car and got Quentin out and walked up to the porch where his mom and grandma were sitting.

They could tell I had been crying, and they asked what happened, so I told them about our fight and me packing his stuff up. I told them I thought he had gone to their house, so I was there to talk to him. Joe's grandma hugged me and told me to think about the reasons we fell in love. His mom told me to sit down with her on the porch so I could relax and calm down.

They could tell I had been crying, and they asked what happened, so I told them about our fight and me packing his stuff up. I told them I thought he had gone to their house, so I was there to talk to him. Joe's grandma hugged me and told me to think about the reasons we fell in love. His mom told me to sit down with her on the porch so I could relax and calm down.

About an hour later, Joe showed up there. He didn't say a word to me and walked past me on the porch and walked inside. We made eye contact as he walked up the porch, and he looked pretty livid, so I didn't say anything to him.

He came outside a little later, and we talked for a few minutes.

"I'm sorry for packing your stuff up and telling you I wanted you out."

I was trying not to cry while we talked, but I felt like breaking down and crying again. I wasn't sure why I was even so upset.

"I don't know why you would do something like that. Now I am not sure if it is a good idea for us to stay together," Joe said.

"I don't know why I did it. I guess I just kept getting the feeling that you hated me and that you were done with this relationship. You have been so distant, and I didn't know what to do," I said.

I don't know if I was so upset because I felt like I made a mistake by taking things too far or if it was because of how upset he was when he saw his stuff was packed up. His reaction was not what I had expected. Part of me was afraid that he might have gone to meet up with my friend. I was confused, and regardless of how I felt earlier that day, at that moment, I just wanted him to come back with me so we could talk about things and work out what the problem was.

Later that night, I asked Joe if he told my friend what I did and he said no. I told him she showed up and seemed like she already knew what happened, but he said he didn't talk to her. He also didn't seem surprised by what I said, either. That night, we ended up working things out and decided to stay together. We tried to put everything behind us and move forward.

After that day, things were okay for a little while. With my dad's help, we found a house to rent and started moving into our new place. It was an adorable side-by-side duplex out in the country, and it was perfect for what we needed.

We moved in and started slowly getting everything we needed to make it feel like a home. It was a few weeks before we had it furnished, but once it was, it felt like a home. I was so happy to be starting over fresh with Joe by my side.

We moved in and started slowly, getting everything we needed to make it feel like a home. It was a few weeks before we had it furnished, but once it was, it felt like a home. I was so happy to be starting over fresh with Joe by my side.

As the weeks went by, my friend started coming over a lot more, and eventually she started coming over every day. Some days, I only had classes in the morning, so I would be home pretty early. She would come over with her kids, and we would let the kids play while we hung out and talked.

Joe was usually at work when she was over, but some days she would be over for hours and she would still be there when Joe got off of work. After a couple of weeks of that happening, Joe made a comment that he didn't like her being there with her kids when he got off work because he couldn't relax. It made sense, so I mentioned it to her a couple of days later when she came over again. I told her Joe didn't like having people at the house all the time, and she would probably need to leave before he came home.

I thought her reaction to me saying that was kind of odd. She seemed offended, which surprised me. She said that it was rude of him and told me it was my house and he shouldn't be able to tell me when I could have friends over. I thought about it and she wasn't wrong.

It was my house, but I still didn't want him upset when he got off of work. She said she was going to stay there until he got off of work that day just to make a point. I said okay, but she would need to leave once he got home.

Joe came home a couple of hours later, and I remember the look on his face when he walked through the door as if it had happened yesterday. He walked in the door and looked right at my friend and looked annoyed. I thought it was odd he looked that upset, and he didn't say anything to me or even look at me. He walked to the bathroom to shower, and I told my friend she should probably go. Joe didn't mention anything about my friend being there after he got out of the shower, so I figured I must have misread his facial expression when he first walked in the door.

Later that night, I told him how she reacted to me, telling her he didn't want anyone at the house when he got off work. He agreed with me and said it was weird she seemed offended by it.

About a week later, Joe and I got into a fight. It was a small fight, and it was irrelevant enough that I didn't remember what the argument was even about. The next day, my friend asked if she could come over with her kids since we both had the day off from school. I didn't want to hang out with anyone that day, but I didn't want to be rude either. When she asked if she could come over, I told her it was okay.

When she got to my house, she told me she didn't have any gas in her car, and asked if she could borrow some money for gas. I was irritated by her asking that because she had gone out of her way to ask if she could come over, and then drove to my house knowing she didn't have money for gas.

I considered her a good friend, though, and I couldn't tell her no. After I gave her some money, I told her not to worry about paying me back.

I wanted to smoke a cigarette, so I told her to come sit on the back porch with me.

We had the kids come outside too, so they could play in the backyard. We stayed on the porch and talked. I told her about the fight Joe and I had the day before, and told her I was still upset over that.

After I told her that, she very matter of factly said, "I just want you to know I would never do anything with Joe or try anything with him."

The comment was so random, and had nothing to do with what I had been talking about, but I thought maybe I was reading too much into it. Maybe she was just being a good friend, and letting me know I can trust her.

I told her, "Thank you," and changed the subject. I told her we should go back inside to hang out.

I replayed that interaction over and over in my head for days after. I wasn't sure what she meant by what she said, but I tried to let it go.

That next Sunday, when Joe was in the bathroom, his cell phone went off, and I picked it up. I saw he had a text from his Aunt Mel.

As I looked at it, I found it strange that his aunt had texted him with just a simple 'hey'. I thought it was weird he spelled her name wrong in his contacts, too.

I opened the text message. At the bottom of the text was a signature with my friend's name, and my heart stopped.

I knew what it was instantly because on one of my older cell phones; I had programmed a signature into my texts so it would show a message at the bottom of each text.

I opened the contact information for his aunt and looked at the phone number and saw that it was my friend's phone number.

I felt a wave of panic washed over me. A sudden wave of intense heat spread throughout my body. A sense of panic rose in my chest, my heart pounding and my breath coming in short, shallow gasps.

I walked into the bathroom, and Joe was standing at the sink.

I held up his phone showing the text, 'hey', with my friend's name below it. Joe looked at his phone and instantly turned red and froze.

I looked at him and said, "Why the fuck is she texting you '*hey*?"

He looked right at me and, with a simple lie, said, "I don't know."

I responded and said, "Why is her number programmed in your phone as Aunt Mel?"

He responded again with the same lie. "I don't know."

I started crying. "Are you cheating on me?"

"No, of course I'm not!"

"Why did she text you, '*hey*', and why are there no other texts from her but that one?"

Joe swore to me he didn't know why she texted that. I asked him why he had her in his phone under another name.

He looked at me with sorrowful eyes and disappointment.

"I don't know Sheila. I guess I just didn't want you to get upset if you saw I had her as a contact in my phone."

"Why would you think I would be upset if you weren't doing anything wrong?" I asked him.

"I'm sorry, I guess I wasn't thinking," Joe said. "I swear to you it's nothing. I really don't know why she texted me."

As the words left his lips, I could see in his eyes, every word was a lie.

I didn't want to believe it, but I knew with every inch of my body that he had been cheating on me with her. It made complete sense, and everything leading up to that day started coming together; the day she showed up at the camper and already knew I packed his stuff up, the days and days she would come over and hang out and stay for hours until Joe got off of work.

I thought about the comment she made about how she would never do anything with Joe. I remembered all the times in the last month Joe would make late night trips to the store and be gone for over an hour even though it took ten minutes to get to the store.

I thought about the constant fighting between us after we moved into the new house. I remembered the comments my friend had made since the house fire about how she didn't think Joe was treating me right and that I should leave him.

Every moment added up, and I realized in that moment that she was trying to take Joe from me.

There are probably a million things I could have done in those moments and hours after seeing that text on Joe's phone, but the only sure thing I decided to do was not let her win. I was not about to walk away from Joe and let her win, even though a huge part of me wanted to tell him to get the hell out of my life and never come back.

I tried to get Joe to tell me the truth over the next couple of months, but he never caved. Every time I brought it up, he said nothing ever happened. He finally gave me a little more and told me she tried to get him to come to her house when her husband wasn't home, but he swore he never did. I could tell he was lying from the way his voice wavered.

I tried to put it behind me and forget the whole situation ever happened. The disappointment I felt was overwhelming. Two people I believed cared about me ended up betraying me.

For a multitude of reasons, I stayed and just tried to move forward with my life and our relationship, even though I knew the relationship was now built on lies. I knew I may never trust him again.

After all of that happened, I started spending more time with my two best friends from high school, Mona and Shelly. I had not spent much time with either of them since I made my move to the new house.

Being back in their presence and talking to them as if we had never spent any time apart made me feel like I was right where I belonged. They were my two closest friends, and I could always count on them for support. No matter the situation, I was always aware that these two were the only ones who would love me unconditionally. I knew they cared for me beyond words.

I gave them a full explanation about what had occurred between my other friend and Joe. They were both furious with Joe and my other friend. They said that Joe was no good for me, and that I should find someone who deserves me. I wanted to listen to their advice, but I felt a wave of guilt sweep over me for considering leaving the life we had been building together. I was not ready to let it go that easily.

As I spent more time with Mona and Shelly, I could feel my worries and sadness melting away. They both brought out the best of me in every situation, and they were always so supportive and uplifting. Joe and I began to rekindle our relationship and connect again.

With some effort, we began to share more experiences and laugh together. We had reached a point in our lives where every day felt like a monotonous routine, and the boredom had begun to weigh us down. We found ways to bring more excitement and happiness into our relationship. As I started to fall in love with him again, I felt my heart grow warmer, but I still held a part of me back, not knowing if we could get back to where we were before.

Months went by and we started talking about having a baby together. I wanted to have another child, and I had always wanted to have my kids in my twenties. I was ecstatic that Joe was on board and wanted to start a family with me.

Every month, I would take a pregnancy test with anticipation, only to have it come back negative. Month after month, I took the test, and the tears streamed down my face as I looked at the negative sign. In the blink of an eye, six months had gone... and then an entire year.

Each month, it got harder on me to see the results. I didn't understand what was wrong with me and why I was not pregnant yet. Despite being on birth control, I conceived Quentin within a year of dating his father, Matt. I had been off of birth control since we had our house fire almost a year and a half ago, and I didn't understand why God would not just let me have what I wanted.

As the weeks and months went on, Joe and I had more and more arguments. Our relationship wasn't in a great place. I started wondering if maybe the reason I had not gotten pregnant yet was because I was not supposed to have a child with him. I wanted so badly to have a child then, because we were in a new home and in a better place with our lives. If we were going to have a baby, I felt like we needed to do it soon.

I had already completed my two year Associates of Science degree and graduated. I had already re-enrolled at the same college for Mechanical Engineering. The classes I had were amazing. I felt like the engineering field would be something I would really love. The classes were harder, and I was under a lot more stress. Maybe that was part of the reason we fought so much.

A couple of months after I started college again, I started what I thought was my period. At first, it seemed like I was just having my period, but then I had intense cramping. It was beyond anything I had ever felt with a period. When I used the bathroom, large clots of blood came out. I was scared because that had never happened before.

The next day, the pain in my uterus was so intense I couldn't get out of bed, and I could barely walk when I did get out of bed. I laid in bed most of the day, crying from the pain. Every time I went to the bathroom, more clots came out. I ended up missing school the entire week. The pain was so intense that I could barely move out of bed for several days.

I bled for almost two weeks.

For the first week, there was such heavy clotting and intense pain that I couldn't do anything but lie in bed, getting up only when I had to. I never went to the doctor because I didn't have a doctor at that time, and I didn't have insurance.

Joe knew something wasn't right.

Joe and I both suspected that I might have had a miscarriage, and I could see the sadness in his eyes. Eventually, the bleeding stopped, but the experience left me feeling drained and uncertain about my future fertility.

Months had passed, and we started trying again. Our relationship was in a better place, and we weren't fighting like we had been before.

Later, in the fall of 2014, I started feeling lightheaded and nauseous, but I was not sure if I was just getting ready to start my period. When I took the pregnancy test, my heart raced as I looked down and saw the two pink lines. I had taken so many pregnancy tests over the last year, and after seeing so many negative tests, I wasn't expecting to be pregnant.

I felt a range of emotions wash over me as I sat there looking at the pregnancy test. Joe and I had been through a lot in the last year and a half. We had a lot of downs, but things were finally getting better. I couldn't wait to see Joe after work to tell him.

That day, I didn't have class, and I drove Joe to work that morning since we lived down the street from his work. When I picked him up after work, I told him I took a pregnancy test and that it was positive. He looked completely shocked and a little scared at the same time. He was happy though, and Joe told me that was excited, but kind of scared.

A few months later, it was time to find out the sex of the baby. When it came time to find out the sex of the baby, we opted for a gender reveal party.

I had always imagined myself as a mother of boys, and the thought of having a daughter filled me with anxiety.

As a victim of sexual abuse and other traumas, I worried about how I could protect my daughter from similar experiences.

After I came became an adult, I started realizing that I had made a huge mistake by not telling anyone about what happened to my in foster care.

The guilt lived inside of me and each year; it grew. What Cain did to me was terrible and unforgivable, but what I did was even worse. I kept silent, holding the secret inside of me for most of my life. As a child and a teenager, I did not realize that keeping that secret could hurt someone else.

It never occurred to me until much later in my life that there was a possibility that I was not the only victim. *Were there girls before me that Cain hurt? Were there any after me? It became more of a possibility, since I never told anyone. How would anyone know that home was not a safe place?*

I am more hurt by my actions than what Cain did to me. I wish it had been something I had known about as a child, because I did not know that the guilt of not telling anyone would consume like it had. My mom had tried to comfort me over the years and remind me that as a five-year-old girl, it was not my responsibility to know I was supposed to tell someone.

That guilt can't rest solely on my shoulders because it could have happened again after I left that house. If it happened again, it was out of control. I know it is not really my fault, but it doesn't stop the guilt from boiling over the surface sometimes.

I hated myself for years for not telling anyone, and even as I hated myself, I still couldn't bring myself to talk about it or tell anyone. It took several more years into my adulthood before I could start giving my mom details and hints about what I went through. The shame and embarrassment kept me silent for so many years.

When the gender reveal finally came, and we learned we were having a girl, I felt a rush of conflicting emotions. When I realized a daughter was joining our family, I felt a rush of happiness, followed by a wave of uncertainty and fear.

I had never been particularly girly myself and wondered if my daughter would resent me for not being able to teach her the "right" things. As the months went on, my worries only grew, and I found myself increasingly uncertain about how to prepare for this new chapter of my life.

The rest of my pregnancy went as planned. And on August 10, 2015, I went into the hospital for my scheduled C-section. Within an hour of being at the hospital, my daughter Nellie was born. She was absolutely perfect in every single way. She had the most beautiful face I had ever seen before, and I was instantly in love with her.

It was a while before I could hold her myself because I was still in surgery, but when I got back to my room, Nellie was waiting for me with her dad. I was able to finally hold her in my arms for the first time. At that moment, I didn't know how I could ever love her more.

I was in the hospital for the next two days, and although this C-section was much better than my first, I still struggled with the recovery. I was finally able to start walking on my own, and the doctor discharged us to go home. Once we were back home, I cried so much. I was terrified to be home from the hospital, and I was not ready to take care of Nellie on my own without help from nurses. She was so much smaller than when her brother Quentin had been born, and she seemed so delicate and frail that I was afraid of hurting her.

Joe did amazing helping with Nellie, and everything seemed to come so naturally to him. He had told me when his son Cole was born; he was even smaller than Nellie, so her being so tiny did not faze him at all.

In the following days, my emotions remained unchanged, and tears flowed non-stop for no apparent reason. I suspected that postpartum depression played a role. There were moments when I couldn't explain my tears. Despite Joe's efforts, I remained inconsolable, and I felt terrible for burdening him with my emotional outbursts. As the days passed, my condition improved, but I still broke down at random moments.

One day, while sitting at the dining table, I watched Quentin playing with Joe on the back porch. I watched from the dining table, overwhelmed with emotion. The sun's warmth coming in from the glass door spread across my skin.

I breathed in, and the sweet newborn smell from Nellie overpowered me. I looked down at her, and my heart felt so full. All of my doubts and fears had dissipated, replaced with a deep sense of gratitude for the family I had.

I smiled as I watched Quentin and Joe play, knowing that they were both safe and loved. And as Nellie snuggled in my arms, her tiny hands wrapped around my finger, I felt complete.

"I love you so much, baby girl."

At that moment, I knew everything had fallen into place.

However, as I gazed down at my daughter, tears started rolling down my cheeks for some reason. Gasping for air, I felt a tightness in my chest. This was what I had always wanted - a family to call my own.

Despite the challenges and tears, everything had come full circle. And as the sun set on that perfect day, I knew that we were meant to be together.

There had been so many times over the years that I feared I would turn into Beverly. I had so many fears that my life would play out much like hers despite my efforts to fight against that. There were days when I could see Beverly coming out of me, and I forced myself to push through it each time. I pushed that version of me deep down inside of me. I realized as I held Nellie in my arms; I had done it.

I was nothing like Beverly.

There was nothing in this world that I wouldn't do for my children. There was nothing I would not sacrifice for them, and I knew as that thought came to me, I was only me.

I was exactly who I was made to be, and exactly who I had fought so hard to become.

I was ready to face whatever challenges lay ahead, knowing that I had my family by my side. With a renewed sense of purpose and hope, I closed my eyes, soaking in the warmth of the sun and the laughter of Quentin.

For the first time in a long time, I felt at peace.

Author Bio

 *Sheila Ruby is a data analyst and author of "A Brief Silence," a memoir that explores the power of perseverance, resilience, and the human spirit in the face of adversity. After serving four years in the Marine Corps, Sheila pursued her education, earning an Associates of Science and an Associates of Applied Science in Mechanical Engineering. Throughout her life, Sheila has faced numerous challenges, from overcoming childhood trauma to navigating the complexities of military service and motherhood. Through it all, she has maintained a deep passion for storytelling and writing, which ultimately led her to write her memoir. In "A Brief Silence," Sheila shares her personal story and offers a powerful message of hope and healing for anyone who has ever faced adversity. Sheila lives in Northwest Ohio with her two children and enjoys exploring new places with them whenever she can.*

Printed in the USA
CPSIA information can be obtained
at www.ICGtesting.com
LVHW031318060823
754248LV00008B/980

9 781088 153871